THE
WESTI
FRONT
FROM THE
AIR

THE WESTERN FRONT FROM THE AIR

NICHOLAS C. WATKIS

FOREWORDS BY
JANE CARMICHAEL, IMPERIAL WAR MUSEUM,
AND GROUP CAPTAIN THORNBER, DIRECTOR, DGIFC

For Jane, Andrew and Katherine for their support in this project.

This book is dedicated to the memory of my grandfather, Francis Benjamin Watkis (1882–1969), Corporal 3rd Battalion The Suffolk Regiment, and my father, 'Jon' Reginald Watkis MPS (1915–1980) Sergeant Pilot RAFVR.

Also to the memory of the gallant photo reconnaissance aircrews of the Royal Flying Corps and the Royal Air Force, 1914–1918.

Cover illustrations. Front: Farman Experimental (FE) 2d from No. 20 Squadron assigned to the Fighting Reconnaissance mission on the Western Front. *Background front*: First known image of Amiens. *Back*: Aerial photograph of Bullecourt. (Medmenham Collection, Intelligence Museum, DISC Chicksands)

First published 1999 by Sutton Publishing Ltd
Second edition published 2000 by Wrens Park Publishing, an imprint of W.J. Williams & Son Ltd

This new edition published 2013
by Spellmount, an imprint of The History Press

The Mill, Brimscombe Port
Stroud, Gloucestershire, GL5 2QG
www.thehistorypress.co.uk

© Nicholas C. Watkis, 1999, 2000, 2013

The right of Nicholas C. Watkis to be identified as the Author of this work has been asserted in accordance with the Copyright, Designs and Patents Act 1988.

British Library Cataloguing in Publication Data.
A catalogue record for this book is available from the British Library.

ISBN 978 0 7524 9777 8

Typesetting and origination by The History Press
Printed in Great Britain

CONTENTS

ACKNOWLEDGEMENTS

I am indebted to Jane Carmichael, Assistant Director Collections, Imperial War Museum, for her assistance and support in preparing this book.

Thanks are also due to the following for their generous help: Hilary Roberts, Head of Collection Managements, Photographic Archive, Imperial War Museum; Colin Bruce, Department of Maps, Imperial War Museum; Peter Chasseaud, specialist in trench maps; David Oxlee OBE, Joint School of Photographic Interpretation, DISC Chicksands, who originally introduced me to the fascination of photographic interpretation and assisted in sourcing the historical material; Mr G.C. Streatfield, Soldiers of Gloucestershire Museum; Steven Gough, the Western Front Association; Martin Fundrey; and S.E. Bennell.

Additional thanks to Terry Finnegan (Col USAF Retd) and Tim Slayter for their assistance in this revised edition.

AUTHOR'S NOTE

In researching my late grandfather's war history, I became interested in discovering what the battlefields of the Western Front were really like. Most photographs and films of the time were taken before or after the action and often from behind the line, and although observation post photography gave a better impression it was still limited.

Having been involved in photographic interpretation, I realised that air reconnaissance photographs would provide a unique insight into the topography, conditions and intelligence of the battles, providing a perspective that had last been seen by the Intelligence Officers at the time, over eighty years ago.

During the process of selecting and evaluating the prints for this book, the high level of skill in interpretation which was achieved by the photo interpreters of the time quickly became apparent; indeed, their skills were no less than those achieved in the Second World War or even those used today.

A NOTE ON THE PHOTOGRAPHS

The original prints are on glass negatives, which are 5 x 4in. The height given for each picture is calculated by the height at which the original photograph was taken. Except where otherwise stated, the camera focal length is 8in. (This remained constant until 1918, when an 8.5in focal length camera was used.)

From mid-1916 onwards, some prints carry a compass 't' to indicate north, but this does not appear to have become standard until 1918. Wherever practical, the photographs have been orientated so that the shadows fall towards the observer, in order that shell-holes appear as depressions rather than mounds. In some cases therefore, to ensure easier viewing, photographs appear to have been printed 'inverted'.

FOREWORD TO THE FIRST EDITION

by Jane Carmichael

Former Assistant Director, Collections
Imperial War Museum

The Imperial War Museum holds enormous collections of objects, documents, film, photographs, sound recordings and works of art detailing the history of conflict from 1914 to the present day. It is very satisfying when enthusiasm and expertise are brought to bear on an area of these collections which results in a fresh interpretation. Nicholas Watkis has done this in taking the Museum's collection of First World War aerial reconnaissance photographs as the starting point for his book. He has been able to use his skill as a fully qualified photographic interpreter and his historical expertise to 'read' these eighty-year-old operational photographs and place them in their proper context as part of the narrative of the struggle on the Western Front.

Historical and fictional accounts of the war in the air during the First World War have concentrated on the glamour of aerial combat and the names of many air 'aces' retain a high popular currency. But the origins of such combat lay in the basic duty of the Royal Flying Corps (later the Royal Air Force) crews to reconnoitre and observe for the benefit of the infantry and artillery, and the enemy's efforts to impede or stop them. Without observers there would have been no aces, and Nicholas Watkis reminds us that the observers and photographers, compilers of aerial records, were subject not only to the predatory instincts of enemy 'scout' fighters but were often exposed to the vagaries of artillery fire from the ground. This took the form of apparently random anti-aircraft fire (nicknamed 'Archie') and the equally terrifying erratic conjunctions with barrage shelling, when aeroplane and shells temporarily shared identical altitudes and trajectories. The aircraft used for aerial photography were flimsy and vulnerable; simply to fly them required a singular dedication and commitment. Nicholas Watkis provides a very welcome tribute to the bravery and endurance demonstrated by the crews of the aerial reconnaissance units in the course of their day-by-day duties of intelligence gathering. He also highlights the invaluable work done by the pioneers of aerial photographic interpretation, whose skilled and painstaking contributions to the overall intelligence picture, are less well known. Their work can now be seen, in very real terms, as the foundation of the precise science of modern aerial photographic interpretation which, as amply demonstrated in this book, became an essential part of operations during the First World War, played a vital role during the Second World War, and which, revolutionised by developments in new technology, continues to play such a vital role in global surveillance today.

December 1998

JANE CARMICHAEL joined the National Museums of Scotland in the newly created post of Director of Collections in July 2003. She is now responsible for its huge range of collections, which include the history of technology, social history, the natural sciences, archaeology, the decorative arts and the history of Scotland. She has led major exhibition projects such as Scotland: A Changing Nation and Silver: Made in Scotland. Jane was the first Director of Collections for the Imperial War Museum in London from 1995 to 2003, where she was responsible for the first IWM website and Collections On-line project. When she ran the IWM Photograph Archive from 1982 to 1995, she specialised in the photography of the First World War.

FOREWORD TO THE NEW EDITION

by Group Captain Steve Thornber MA BSc RAF
Director, Defence Geospatial Intelligence Fusion Centre
RAF Wyton

As we approach the centenary of the Great War, it is appropriate to take a fresh look at how we view this truly tumultuous period in history, its role in the shaping of the busy century that followed, and the importance of both its mistakes and its innovations. While the importance of aerial observation and photography had become apparent as far back as the French Revolution and then the American Civil War, the science and tactics required to use it successfully at scale really came to the fore with the air war over the trenches of Western Europe. In this revision of his book, Watkis has given us a bird's-eye view of the five major Western Front battlefields of the Great War; he adds a fascinating and absorbing dimension to our knowledge, one that really makes us think about the bravery of the reconnaissance aircrew and the ingenuity of those exploiting the photographs. Perhaps the author is able to do this in a way that others cannot, because of his years as a Royal Auxiliary Air Force Reservist Imagery Analyst. With a real empathy for the challenges and urgency facing the people involved at the time, Watkis offers us a very accessible and visual insight into this still quite secretive world. This book is an important accompaniment for anyone trying to get under the skin of the role aerial reconnaissance played in the day-to-day struggle for nothing less than the future of global power at the dawn of the age of technology.

August 2013

INTRODUCTION

This book developed out of a study of the contents of the 'Box Collection' at the Imperial War Museum. This showed that the 'Box Collection' holds a unique view of the First World War, in that it contains the largest known surviving air reconnaissance archive, comprising approximately 150,000 glass negatives from the Western Front and other theatres of war. Although it has been used here to provide particular illustrations, the 'Box Collection' has not been used since 1918 for its original purpose, which was to given an intelligence picture of the battlefields.

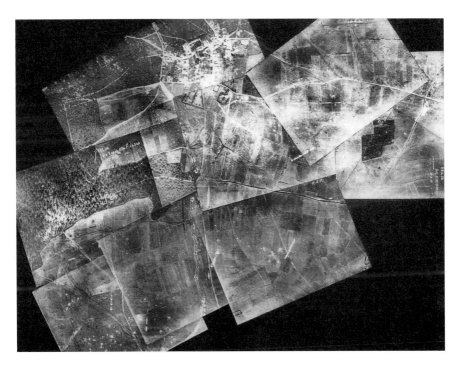

Photographic mosaic for Wagonlieu, map 51c, dated 17 August 1917. (Medmenham Collection, Intelligence Museum, DISC Chicksands)

A dispatch rider handing a message to a mobile photographic processing van. (Medmenham Collection, Intelligence Museum, DISC Chicksands)

The book is not intended to offer a full military history of the selected battles, but rather to show the military conditions of the areas at the time. Each battle is described in outline, and the battlefield illustrated with the relevant part of the contemporary GSGS map. Photographs have been selected from the point of view of an Intelligence Officer, whose primary requirement was information about the enemy dispositions. Because of limitations of space and opportunity, photographs have been included on the basis of relevance and timing, preference being given to those taken just before, during or just after the initial attack took place. Selection was also limited by the availability or otherwise of photographs in the archive records and the negative collection. Surprisingly, few record entries are missing from the negative collection, but there are some apparent gaps in dates; these gaps may perhaps be due to physical loss but it is more likely that weather conditions precluded photography on those dates.

The use of air photography offers a unique approach to the First World War battlefields, showing them as they were at the time of the attack and illustrating topography, conditions, and defences in a manner which is impossible by any other means. They also show how much information could be gathered by air reconnaissance – its potential contribution to the overall strategic and tactical intelligence picture was enormous. Air photography was used for the first time as part of the planned preparation for a battle at Neuve Chapelle in 1915. Its prime purpose then was to support the Royal Engineers field survey sections by providing accurate and up-to-date information for map-making.

RFC mobile reconnaissance/intelligence centre van. (Medmenham Collection, Intelligence Museum, DISC Chicksands)

An observation balloon crew preparing to ascend. Note the camera on the tripod. (Medmenham Collection, Intelligence Museum, DISC Chicksands)

As the war progressed, so the quality and quantity of air photographs increased, and most of those that have been released in recent years date from the late part of the war. It seems appropriate therefore that this study of the battlefields of the Western Front should start with images from the 'Box Collection', beginning at Neuve Chapelle in March 1915.

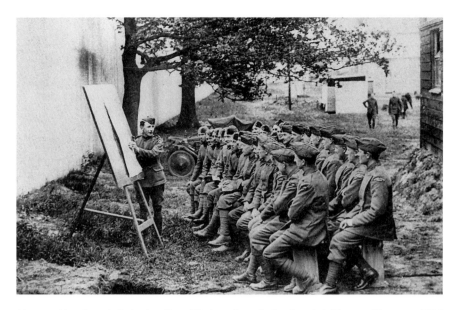

Airmen attending photo instruction. (Medmenham Collection, Intelligence Museum, DISC Chicksands)

A pilot studying an air photograph. (Medmenham Collection, Intelligence Museum, DISC Chicksands)

A C-type camera mounted next to the rear cockpit of a Royal Aircraft Factory BE2c reconnaissance aircraft. (Medmenham Collection, Intelligence Museum, DISC Chicksands)

A BE2c overflies the trenches. Built by the Royal Aircraft Factory, Farnborough, the BE series of biplanes bore the brunt of the first years of the air war in the reconnaissance and light bomber roles. The BE2c had a top speed of 72mph at 6,500ft and carried a crew of two. (Medmenham Collection, Intelligence Museum, DISC Chicksands)

A typical RFC airfield with hangar tents, 1915. This is probably a training airfield, judging by the presence of Farman Longhorn and Shorthorn aircraft. (Medmenham Collection, Intelligence Museum, DISC Chicksands)

HISTORY

The origins of air photo intelligence lie in the beginnings of photography, when the first photograph was reportedly taken in 1827 by a Frenchman, Joseph Nicephore Niépce.

In 1858, Gaspard Felix Tournachon took the first recorded aerial photograph from a balloon that was tethered over the Bievre Valley at an altitude of 262ft. In America, in October 1860, James Wallace Black ascended to an altitude of 1,200ft in a tethered balloon and photographed portions of the city of Boston.

However, the first reported military application of aerial photography is believed to have occurred in 1862 during the Union siege of Richmond, Virginia, when two gridded map-like prints were produced and used by the balloon observers to direct artillery fire. The American Civil War established the need for observation from balloons.

By 1879, there were five balloons in British military service, and they were first used during the Sudan campaign in 1884–85 and the British expedition to Bechaunaland. A balloon section and depot were formed as permanent units of the Royal Engineers establishment.

Niépce – view from studio window.

Above: Black – Boston, 1860.

Left: A vertical aerial photograph of the Balloon School Camp at Lydd in Kent, 1886.

During the South African War (1899–1902), there were four balloon sections
employed in the theatre. Although used only in small numbers to 'look over the
hill', their primary roles were observing enemy troop movements and directing
artillery fire, including a photographic reconniassance section. Air photography
was still in its infancy, but it was recognised that a photograph was better than the

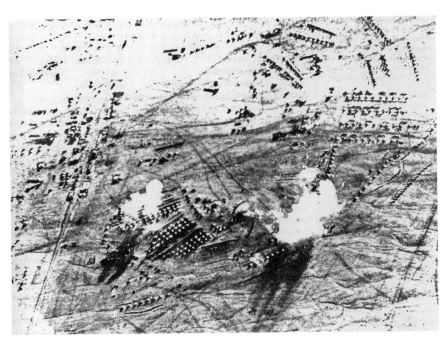

A balloon photograph of a British camp under Boer artillery fire during the South African War
(1899–1902).

The BE2c was widely used for reconnaissance duties over the Western Front, although by 1917
it had been relegated to training and home defence.

'observer's glance' and provided a lasting visual record. Thus, some of the earliest surviving balloon photographs date from the Boer War.

Although aviation developed quickly after 1900, particularly after the Wright brothers' flights, it was not until 1911 that the War Office tentatively adopted the new development, forming the Air Battalion of the Royal Engineers. The battalion consisted of three companies, one each of balloons, small airships and man-lifting kites. Aeroplanes were not initially included but new developments, coupled with the enthusiasm of some military officers who learned to fly privately, caused the War Office to re-form the Air Battalion the following year, 1912, as the Royal Flying Corps (RFC).

A joint service unit with naval and military wings, the RFC was designed to meet the needs of both services, and was equipped with aeroplanes. A Central Flying School was established at Upavon in Wiltshire, which was staffed by officers and men from both services, the Commandant being Geoffrey Paine RN, with Major Hugh Trenchard as the Second-in-Command and Chief Instructor. The RFC was commanded by Brigadier Henderson, an expert in field intelligence and reconnaissance, who considered air photography an important development. Henderson published *The Art of Reconniassance* in

Brigadier
Henderson.

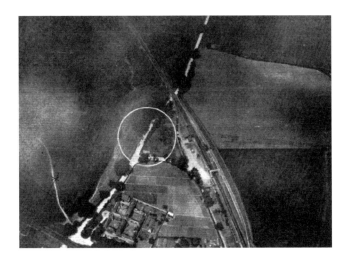

Reconnaissance
target (four wagons)
15 June 1914,
2,000ft.

1907, and by 1914, his work had been published in a third edition, to include a new chapter on aerial reconnaissance.

Experimental work on air photography was carried out at Farnborough, where the majority of the early photographs were oblique, but by mid-1913, experiments were made with a specially designed camera to give vertical overlapping photographs.

In parallel with the photographic work being carried out at Farnborough, the aircrew of 3 Squadron RFC, realising the possible value of aerial photography to military reconnaissance work, purchased their own cameras and adapted them for use in the air. They came up with a system of developing the glass plate negatives in the air so that upon landing they would be ready to print. During the summer manoeuvres of 1913, the squadron tested its techniques and, early in 1914, produced examples of its work. The hand-held, press-type cameras they adapted and used, with a 6in lens, became the camera type used most frequently by the RFC until the introduction of the specially designed 'A' camera in 1915.

From the outset, the military role of the RFC was clearly defined as reconnaissance; they were to seek out the enemy and report on his dispositions. The Admiralty soon decided that it wanted to control its own aircraft and so in July 1914 the Royal Naval Air Service was formed, and the RFC reverted to being a Corps of the Army.

(N.B. Italy became the first nation to use aeroplanes for military purposes during the Italian-Turkish war of 1911–12, when they were used for reconnaissance, leaflet dropping and to drop the first aerial bomb. No evidence has so far been produced of the use of air photography during the campaign.

Immediately after the outbreak of war, the four squadrons of the RFC under General Henderson were sent to France as part of the British Expeditionary Force (BEF), and were soon involved in reconnaissance patrols. Observers made

A unit of mixed aircraft including two BE12s and one RE8.
The BE12 was a single-seat adaptation of the BE2c, intended for use as a fighter. However, heavy losses saw it relegated to second-line duties that included reconnaissance.
The RE8 was the most widely used two-seater on the Western Front, but was an easy target for enemy fighters. It was used for reconnaissance and bombing duties.

in-flight reports on enemy movements and sent their reports to the commanders on the ground on landing. The value of these reports was quickly appreciated and made a substantial contribution to the intelligence picture of the BEF during the retreat from Mons.

It was apparently during the advance from the Marne that the first air photographs of the war were taken. The first five photographs were taken by Lt G. Prettyman of 3 Squadron RFC on 15 September 1914 and showed German gun positions on the River Aisne. At this stage of the war, the impetus for aerial photography innovation rested at the junior officer level.

During the autumn of 1914, although not officially sanctioned to do so, 3 Squadron continued to take photographs, the majority being taken by Lt Charles Curtis Darley, who used his own Aeroplex camera, fitted with a 12in lens. Lt Darley, a Royal Artiller (RA) officer serving as an observer in the 3 Squadron, assembled all the photographic coverage of the German lines on the Fourth Corps front to build up a mosaic of the German defense system. He carried out the interpretation and identified and annotated all the salient points of interest, showing the latest developments in the German defensive positions. The mosaic, completed during January 1915, was intended for use by the squadron for planning and reporting purposes, but the squadron commander, Major J.M. Salmond, was so impressed that he took it to Corps Headquarters. The detail the photographs provided showed the potential value of air photographs as an essential element of battle planning.

Although these photographs were taken privately and unoffically, their value as a pictorial record was quickly appreciated. It therefore did not take long for the value of air photography to result in official recognition and the establishment of an Air Photographic Section.

The first section was founded by Maj. Salmond in January 1915 as part of No. 1 Wing RFC, with Lt J.T.C. Moore Brabazon, Lt C.D.M. Cambell, Flt Sgt F.C.V. Lewis and 2nd Air Mech. W.D. Corse. Their first task was to design an efficient camera; their efforts resulted in the 'A' camera, which was quickly produced to their specification by Thornton Pickard Manufacturing in March 1915. The 'A' camera, first used on 2 March 1915, was hend–held and weighed 10lb. It had an 8in lens, and observers carried six glass plates that were loaded by hand. With the advent of the 'C'-type camera later in 1915, the camera could be fitted to the aircraft on a fixed vertical moun. The 'C' camera retained an 8in lens but carried a magazine of eighteen glass plates that could be loaded automatically.

Examples of photographic pairs from stereo cameras.

This photograph of an artillery bombardment, possibly using gas shells, was taken from a British observation post in the Somme area, probably in 1916.

The BE12 offered an improvement in performance over its predecessor the BE2c, with a maximum speed of 102mph and a service ceiling of 12,500ft. As a fighter the BE12 was still easy prey for faster and more manoeuvrable enemy aircraft so it was quickly reassigned to light bombing and reconnaissance duties late in 1916.

The maps used by the BEF were quickly found to be inadequate and unreliable, being based on two sets of maps, one Belgian and one French. While the Belgian maps were based on a relatively recent survey, the French maps were derived from a Napoleonic one. Thus the Royal Engineers decided that the BEF's area of front should be resurveyed as a matter of urgency. Although the greater part of the 1915 survey was done by standard ground survey methods, there was increasing interest in the use of air photography to assist in map-making.

From these small beginnings, the value of air photography increased dramatically. It helped to correct the tendency for observers to exaggerate their reports, and provided visual proof of reconnaissance claims. Certainly, in the preparation for the Battle of Neuve Chapelle in March 1915, air photography was seen as an important source of intelligence. Photographs could reveal camouflaged positions not visible to an observer, and allowed a more detailed examination of enemy positions than could an air observer.

The growing importance of air photography to the development of intelligence on the Western Front

Right: Wing Commander Hamshaw-Thomas, photographed during the Second World War, when he was recalled for photo-interpretation duties. As a pioneer in the First World War he was responsible for planning and undertaking the mapping of Palestine and for producing the 1:40,000 map for the Battle of Gaza.

Below: A photographic interpreter at work, *c.* 1916. Believed to be Hamshaw-Thomas on the Italian front.

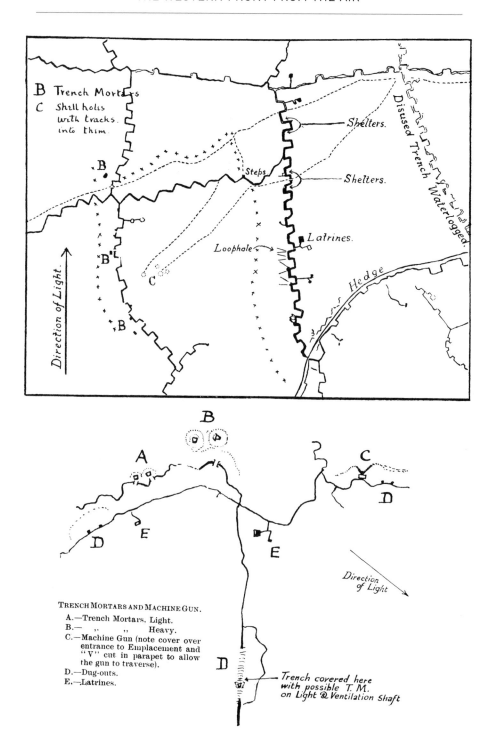

These three illustrations are taken from *Notes on the Interpretation of Aeroplane Photographs,* published in 1916.

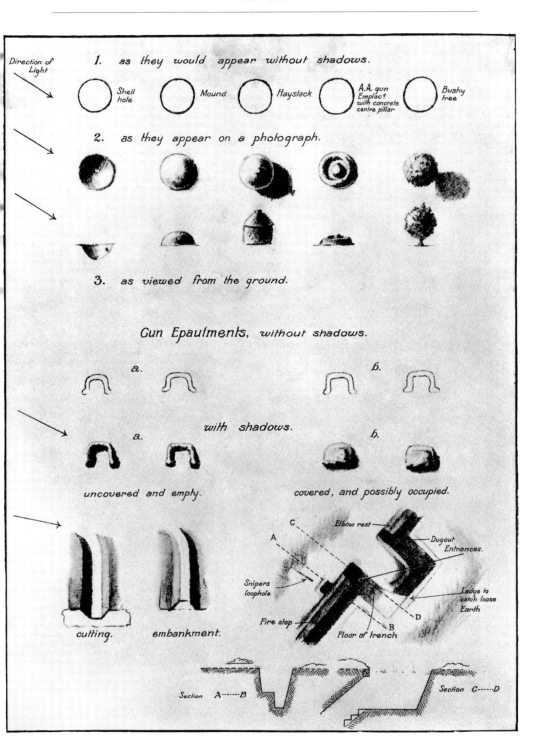

Direction of Light

1. as they would appear without shadows.

Shell hole   Mound   Haystack   A.A. gun Emplac† with concrete centre pillar   Bushy tree

2. as they appear on a photograph.

3. as viewed from the ground.

Gun Epaulments, without shadows.

a.   b.

with shadows.

a.   b.

uncovered and empty.   covered, and possibly occupied.

cutting.   embankment.

Elbow rest
C
A   Dugout Entrances.
Snipers loophole   Ledge to catch loose Earth
Fire step   D
Floor of trench   B

Section A----B   Section C----D

MACHINE GUN EMPLACEMENT.

1. Front and side view, without shadows.

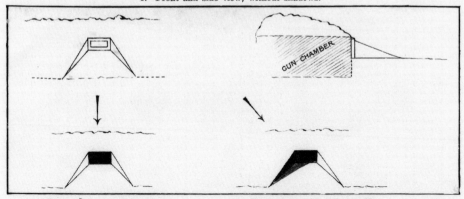

2. Front view, with light above.   3. Front view, with light at side.

DIAGRAM SHOWING PLAN OF CONSTRUCTION, HEAD COVER

AND METHOD OF STORING AMMUNITION, FROM CAPTURED EMPLACEMENTS NEAR FRICOURT.

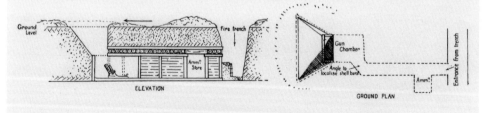

TRENCH MORTAR EMPLACEMENTS, SHOWING DIFFERENCE IN

APPEARANCE ACCORDING TO DIRECTION OF LIGHT.

These two photographs of no-man's-land were taken from the British lines. They epitomise the popular image of First World War battlefields. (Soldiers of Gloucestershire Museum)

Trench conditions. **Above**: a forward trench occupied by the Glosters, 1915. **Below**: a forward trench in the Somme area, late 1916. (Soldiers of Gloucestershire Museum)

was confirmed at the Headquarters of the First Army where Lt Col Chatteris controlled an intelligence staff of two regular and three wartime officers, all employed on photographic interpretation work. One of these wartime officers, Captain Charles Romer, was a barrister and surveyor, and devised the first rules for scaling air photographs. He is now generally regarded as the first true photographic interpreter.

Camera developments continued and the first stereoscopic aerial photographs were taken in early 1915 by Lt Bingham RFC using a modified standard Thornton Pickard camera and an ordinary portable viewer bought in Amiens.

Once air photography had been accepted by the General Staff as a prime and reliable source of intelligence, a School of Photography, Mapping and Reconnaissance was set up at Farnborough in September 1916. The demand for air photographs increased significantly as its importance was realised. During the Battle of the Somme between July and November 1916, the RFC took more than 19,000 air photographs from which 430,000 prints were made. To evaluate this vast number of photographs, extra staff were required and by December 1916 every squadron engaged on reconnaissance duties had been given an intelligence section comprising one Intelligence Officer, two draughtsmen and a clerk. The duties of these intelligence sections were formally laid down by Brig Gen Chatteris, now Head of Intelligence at General Headquarters. Duties included the briefing and debriefing of observers before and after reconnaissance flights; the examination and interpretation of air photographs, and the issuing of information derived from photographs and reports as quickly as possible. The first manual, *Notes on the Interpretation of Aeroplane Photographs*, was published at the end of 1916. Further advances were made with vertical air cameras, including cameras of 20in focal length, being fitted to most reconnaissance aircraft. Progress continued in the use of air photography for mapping notably when Col M.N. McLeod RE devised a system for rectifying aerial photographs used for survey work.

In other theatres of war, aerial photographs were used extensively to produce a 1:40000 scale map for the Battle of Gaza and for mapping the whole of southern Palestine. They were also used extensively in Italy and Mesopotamia. By 1918 the volume of print production was phenomenal. In one week, while German preparations for their March offensive were under way, interpreters examined some 10,440 photographs, and were increasingly employed in directing artillery fire.

The importance of aerial photography can be illustrated by the number of prints produced by the photographic sections during 1918. Some 5,287,000 prints had been made by September, with a further 650,000 produced in October; by 11 November 1918 the total number of prints produced on the Western Front was approaching six million.

Since the end of the First World War the popular and enduring image of the Royal Flying Corps, the Royal Naval Air Service, and the Royal Air Force has been that of the scout or fighter pilot, epitomised by the names Ball, Bishop, Mannock and McCudden. Yet while not wishing to diminish the standing of these famous names, the majority of pilots and observers were involved in some way with reconnaissance. The exploits and bravery of these aircrew have been largely unsung, yet it was their task to carry out the RFC's primary work of reconnaissance over and beyond the enemy's lines, not only on the Western Front but also in the Middle East, the Balkans and Italy. Reconnaissance flying required precision and steady nerves, as the aircraft had to be flown in specific patterns in order to gain the necessary photographic coverage. The principal aircraft in use were the BE2c, 2d and 2e until late 1916 when the RE8 and subsequently the Armstrong Whitworth AK came into service. These aircraft were stable camera platforms, but their stability, coupled with low-powered engines, made them easy targets for enemy fighters. Not only that but their low speeds of around 80 to 90mph meant that in a headwind their ground speed was often reduced to perhaps 40 to 50mph, making them vulnerable to anti-aircraft guns. The height at which the reconnaissance aircraft flew was dictated by the camera's requirements. In many cases it is possible to calculate the aircraft's height from the photographs. However, pilots such as the late Cecil Lewis have reported that some aircraft flew over the Somme as low as 500ft, while others flew at perhaps 4,000–6,000ft, a height at which the aircrew could see shells reaching their maximum trajectory alongside their aircraft before tumbling back towards the ground. Unfortunately, it was not unknown for aircraft to be destroyed in this way by shells from the artillery barrage.

READING AND INTERPRETATION OF AERIAL PHOTOGRAPHS

Air photographs can be examined at several levels. Unlike the air interpreter, the general reader does not seek to extract all the information from the photograph, but only sufficient for his particular interest. All photographs are divided into two types, vertical and oblique. Vertical photographs are taken with a camera pointing straight down, while obliques are taken with the camera at an angle, so that the view is similar to that from a hill-top. Oblique photographs are themselves of two classes: low angle and high angle. The 'angle' refers to the angle of the camera in relation to an imaginary vertical line drawn through the earth.

Generally, the view on a high-angle oblique includes the horizon, whereas a low-angle view does not. Of the 'Box Collection' archive, probably 90 per cent are vertical photographs.

It is important that aerial photographs are viewed correctly. Shadows should fall towards the viewer. This means that shell-holes will appear as depressions. (With the shadows falling away from the viewer, shell-holes appear as small mounds.) The photograph should then be compared with the appropriate map.

IDENTIFICATION OF OBJECTS

There are five principal steps in the identification of objects on air photographs: shape, size, shadow, tone and associated features. Beginners should take each step in the sequence given. With more experience the photo reader will build up a mental 'library' covering all types of objects and patterns, and with practice the eye learns to recognise patterns and immediately notices anything unusual.

Print No. P18V66 24 April 1917 Map 51B SW4: Bullecourt
This is an example of a low-angle oblique. The annotations are those originally applied.
(Medmenham Collection, Intelligence Museum, DISC Chicksands)

Print No. 15ae 1539 24 April 1917 Map 51B SW4: Bullecourt
This is an example of a high-angle oblique. The annotations are those originally applied.
(Medmenham Collection, Intelligence Museum, DISC Chicksands)

Shape: Shape (and perhaps pattern) is the first thing that the eye sees in an air photograph, and it often provides immediate identification. However, many things have similar shape but different size when viewed from a vertical position. For example, static water tanks, gas holders, roundabouts, wells and water towers all have a circular shape but they will be of different sizes:

Size: This can be estimated either by comparison with a known object that can be recognised or by measurement calculated from the scale of the photograph.

Shadow: Shadows on photographs will indicate the height of an object as well as its shape and sometimes its construction. A building may often by identified from the shadow of its roof. Shadows may also show objects that are otherwise hidden, or camouflaged, such as guns or tanks. Photographs taken with a low sun on the horizon show up ground features with particular clarity. In a snow-covered landscape, shadows from a low sun reveal much that would otherwise be hidden. Similarly, a low sun casts shadows that can often reveal 'cropmarks' of otherwise hidden archaeological sites.

Tone: Tone in photographs is related to the texture and colour of an object, and is a measure of the amount of light it reflected back to the camera. The smoother the object, the greater the amount of light reflected back, so that a tarmac road may appear lighter than a green field or grass. Moisture in the ground will affect tone by darkening exposed earth and showing more luxuriant vegetation.

Associated features: Often objects can be identified by the associated features around them. For example, a circular pond might be in a field, while a circular roundabout would be at a road junction. In the identification of military objects, the main associated features are often tracks, emplacements and trenches. Each type of military equipment requires a differently shaped pit, usually to a standard pattern, and the photo interpreter soon learns to distinguish distinctive patterns to identify them.

STEREO PHOTOGRAPHS

The principal advantage of stereo photography is that it provides a three-dimensional view and allows the perception of shape, size and position of the ground and of objects that cannot be seen on a single photograph. The air cameras of the First World War were plate cameras that required an exchange of glass plates. Initially plates were changed by hand between each exposure, but wtih the advent of the 'C' camera in late 1915, plates could be changed automatically, making a 'run of prints' over a target theoretically possible. However, because of the need to obtain a 60 per cent overlap from successive photo frames to obtain effective stereo pairs, it was usually impossible to

Prints Nos 4AE1665 and 1666 26 March 1917 Map 57c NE1 Queant
These photographs show the German lines to the west of Bourlon. The lower print appears to belong to a 'run' of prints taken for stereo overlap, although the overlap here is less than the usual 60 per cent.

obtain a genuine three-dimensional photograph. During the First World War, most stereo photographs appear to have been taken with a stereo camera, used for photographing specific installations. From the surviving imagery, it would seem that the RNAS used them more than the RFC. However, later in the war cameras with automatic plate change enabled 'runs' of prints to be taken, thus producing stereo pairs. (See the pair of prints overleaf.)

A BRIEF INTRODUCTION TO THE GSGS (GEOGRAPHIC SECTION GENERAL STAFF) MAP SERIES

GSGS Series 3062 scale: 10,000
GSGS Series 2742 scale: 20,000
GSGS Series 2743 scale: 40,000

The map grid system was based on the 1:40,000 scale artillery maps. These maps were divided up into areas 6,000 yards square, which were identified by capital letters *A* to *X*. These areas were subdivided into thirty-six numbred 1,000-yard squares, which in turn were subdivided into four lettered (lowercase) 500-yard squares: *a*, *b*, *c*, *d*. Points within the 500-yard squares were pinpointed by four-figure coordinates, eastings and then northings.

A full grid reference would thus read (sheet number first): 28.S.17.D.4730.

These references were identical for the 1:20,000 and the 1:10,000 maps, as these were regarded as subdivisions of the 1:40,000 sheets.

TITLING STRIP – INFORMATION FOUND ON THE EDGE OF PRINTS

Every print found in the Box Collection has a unique titling strip of information along the edge. With prints from the early years, the titling information is fairly simple but became progressively more detailed as time went on.

EXAMPLE:
Titling Strip: 5AE 25   7.8.18 7am F8 ¼ 62D V   25bd 26ac

5AE	negative series number
25	local serial of the print
7.8.18 7am	date, time of image
F8 ¼	focal length of camera

62D	map sheet number
V	identification of the 6,000-yard square
25bd 26ac	identification of the 500-yard squares or parts thereof covered by the photographic print

(N.B. Where north is indicated on a print, it is denoted by a 't' with the top of the 't' pointing north.)

NEUVE CHAPELLE

10TH TO 12TH MARCH 1915

In early 1915 it was uncertain whether the bulk of the forces of the British Empire would be used in Northern France or would be sent to other 'promising' theatres in the Near East or along the Belgian coast. To 'clear the air' Sir John French deemed it necessary that there should be some action in France that would justify priority for the French theatre and his command there. Haig's view was that, supplied with ample high-explosive artillery ammunition, 'we could walk through the German lines at several places'.

The battle plan for Neuve Chapelle was based on the need to make a significant impact, not only to convince the War Cabinet of the importance of the Western Front but also to demonstrate to General Joffre the BEF's determination and ability. The plan was essentially a tactical offensive, making use of superiority of numbers and the element of surprise, to break the German line and inflict a sharp reverse.

In the spring of 1915, after a wet winter, the Germans had reduced their forces in the west, diverting men and artillery to support their fresh offensives on the Eastern Front. This was especially true of the British sector of the Front, where the Germans believed the British to be incapable of any effective offensive action. This was particularly noticeable in the area around Neuve Chapelle. Here the German line formed a salient, about 2,000yds deep, around and in front of the ruined village of Neuve Chapelle, between the Moated Grange and Port Arthur. Defended by some 1,400 men and twelve machine guns, the position was exposed to fire from three sides. Trench works consisted of a single line of sandbagged breastworks built shoulder-high on waterlogged ground, and protected by wire on portable *chevaux de Frise*.

To attack this salient, Haig proposed an order of battle comprising forty-eight battalions (about 40,000 men), supported by sixty-two batteries of 18-pounders, with forty 4.5in howitzers and eighty-two siege and heavy guns for counter-battery fire. Behind the attack would be the Cavalry Corps and the Indian Cavalry Corps. Enemy forces were accurately established, including the existence of a reserve force consisting of a machine-gun company and 800 infantry some 4 miles behind the line at Ligny-le-Grand. In addition, the German forces had about 4,000 infantry within twelve hours of Neuve Chapelle, with a further 16,000 available within forty-eight hours from reserves based around Lille.

Preparation for the battle began at the end of February. The troops selected to take part were from the Fourth Corps under Lt Gen. Sir Harold Rawlinson, and the Indian Corps under Sir John Willcock. On the British left, to the north of the Moated Grange, was the 7th Division, with the 8th Division in the centre, and the Meerut Division on the right. Preparation was thorough. Models of the battlegrounds were constructed in the rear area and troops were rehearsed in the details. Aerial photography was used for the first time as part of the intelligence planning, providing details of the enemy lines and preparing maps of the trench systems, which were issued to officers for the first time.

On the eve of the assault, rain fell steadily, with occasional flurries of snow. The temperature was just above freezing. The ground was sodden and the communication trenches waterlogged. Despite the weather, the attacking

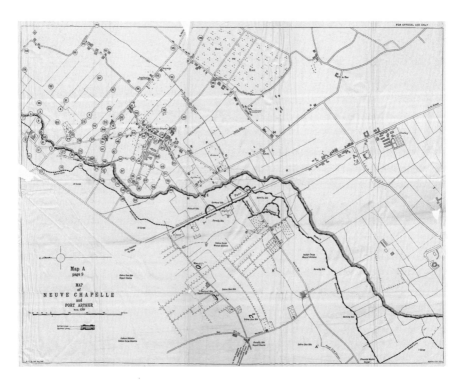

This planning map was produced from the annotated photograph shown above. The reference points relate to the Operational Orders for the attack on 10 March 1915. (National Archives)

This annotated photograph is the earliest known surviving air photograph taken by the RFC during the war. It was probably taken with a press-type camera, in early February 1915, specifically for the planning of the offensive at Neuve Chapelle. (National Archives)

battalions moved up to their jumping-off positions during the night, and were assembled by 04.30 hours.

Despite the number of guns available for the opening bombardment and the relative narrowness of the front, little damage was inflicted on the enemy breastworks on the extreme left, as the 58th and 81st Siege Batteries which were

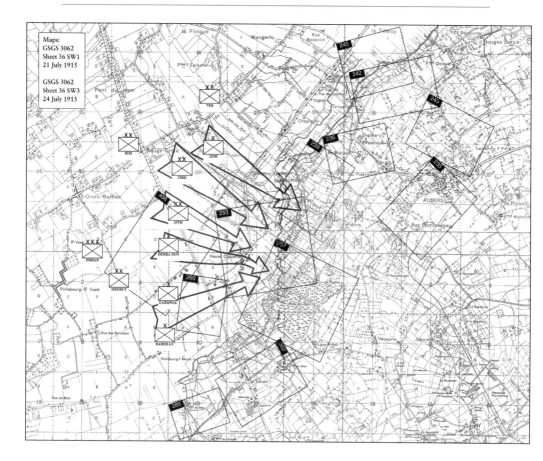

Maps:
GSGS 3062
Sheet 36 SW1
21 July 1915

GSGS 3062
Sheet 36 SW3
24 July 1915

to undertake the task only arrived the evening before the assault and they were not in position to take part in the bombardment the following day.

The artillery bombardment began at 07.30 hours on 10 March, with a hurricane bombardment lasting thirty-five minutes on a frontage of only 1,200yds. This was the strongest concentration of guns per yard ever assembled, giving an intensity of artillery fire that would not be equalled again until 1917 at Ypres.

At 08.45 hours the barrage had lifted and moved 300yds further east. This was the signal for the assaulting troops to climb out of their trenches and advance across the muddy fields of no-man's-land towards the German lines.

The frontage between Signpost Lane and the road leading to the village, a distance of some 400yds, was attacked by the 25th Brigade. The wire had been cut by the bombardment, allowing the brigade to cross the German line with relatively few losses as the enemy had been completely demoralised by the artillery fire. Having achieved the enemy front line the brigade continued to advance to the German support trenches less than 100yds to the rear. When the leading battalions were halted, the support battalions passed through them and went forward to occupy the village, which was captured shortly before

09.00 hours. The brigade then waited until the artillery barrage moved on to the area between the Bois du Biez and the village.

On the left of the 25th Brigade, the leading battalions of the 23rd Brigade attacked immediately north of Signpost Lane in order to establish a front along the Armentières Road. This was the area designated for the two 6in howitzer batteries. However, owing to delays in leaving England, the batteries were late into position and consequently had problems in target registration. This resulted in an inadequate bombardment which left the enemy trenches and wire largely intact. Thus the leading waves of both the 2nd Middlesex and the 2nd Scottish Rifles attacked a fully defended and virtually undamaged position, where they were met by heavy rifle and machine-gun fire and were effectively destroyed. Of the 700 or so men of the 2nd Middlesex who took part in the assault, more than 400 were killed or wounded.

On the right of the British line was the Indian Corps, consisting of the Dehra Dun Brigade on the left and the Garhwal Brigade on the far right around the village of Port Arthur. The Garhwal troops attacked with mixed results. The battalions attacking Neuve Chapelle itself faced little opposition as the wire had been largely destroyed by the artillery bombardment. The first objective had been the old Smith-Dorrien trench which lay about 300yds east of the village; this was reached by about 09.00 hours. Unfortunately, the brigade attack south of Port Arthur was less successful. The leading companies of the assault battalion, the 1/39 Garhwals, lost direction and swung off to the right of their intended path, running into German defences that had not been targeted by the artillery fire plan. Although under heavy fire and sustaining heavy casualties (all their British officers were killed), the Garhwalis captured the trench.

The main problem that faced the BEF at Neuve Chapelle was the failure of the artillery to destroy enough of the German wire and trenches. The late arrival of the 6in howitzer battery and its failure to register its allocated targets in front of the 23rd Brigade, combined with the field artillery's inability to destroy the wire, caused the advance in this sector to come to a standstill when the leading battalions of the Scottish Rifles and the Middlesex sustained severe casualties. In addition, communications went from bad to worse as the field telephone lines, which had been laid in duplicate and triplicate, were repeatedly cut by the German artillery fire. This increasingly resulted in information having to be transmitted and relayed by runners, and all too frequently messages failed to get through, as runners were killed, or were so delayed because of battle conditions that the information was seriously out of date by the time it was received.

Neuve Chapelle was captured by 13.00 hours, and the artillery barrage between the village and the Bois du Biez prevented enemy counter-attacks. Until this time, the main attack around the salient of the village itself had been undertaken by the Garhwal Brigade of the Indian Corps and the 23rd and 25th Brigades of the 8th Division.

The 7th Division sector was to the north-east of Neuve Chapelle, where the German line straightened out beyond the Moated Grange. The attack here was led by the 22nd Brigade, although they were not involved in the morning's initial assault. Supporting the 22nd were the 21st and 20th Brigades, which were still in reserve a mile behind the British front lines. Poor communications left General Rawlinson unaware that the 'Orchard' – a key point in the German defence line – had been captured shortly before midday. It was therefore over an hour later, at 13.15 hours, that the 21st Brigade received orders from General Rawlinson to prepare to advance towards the Aubers Ridge, as soon as the 24th Brigade was in position. Although the attack was initially timed for 14.00 hours, Rawlinson decided to synchronise the attack with that of the Indian Corps in the Port Arthur sector and therefore rescheduled the attack for 14.50 hours. He ordered the 24th Brigade to advance to the village of Le Pietre, while the 21st Brigade was to move towards the Rue d'Enfer. The objectives of both these units had escaped serious damage by the British artillery fire, and poor communications resulted in serious delays in the assembly of both brigades. It was therefore not until 17.30 hours, as the daylight was fading, that the attack commenced; the troops advancing several hundred yards before being forced to stop by heavy machine-gun fire.

In the Port Arthur salient, the Indian Corps suffered similar problems and delays. When the Dehra Dun Brigade finally received the order to advance to the Bois du Biez, there were further delays before the brigade's leading battalions began to move along the Edgware Road, before turning south-east towards the Bois du Biez. The lead battalion reached the wood at about 18.30 hours and came under strong enfilade machine-gun fire from the German strongpoint around the Layes Bridge; at the same time, German reinforcements were entering the wood from the east. The Dehra Dun Brigade commander, anxious to avoid the confusion of fighting in the dark, decided to withdraw to a position behind the Layes Brook, particularly as he was aware that the advance by the 7th and 8th Divisions had been halted.

Although General Haig had received intelligence of German reinforcements during the day, he underestimated the numbers and gave orders for the attack to be resumed the following day, 11 March. The Indian Corps was to advance through the Bois du Biez, while on their left the 7th and 8th Divisions were to advance toward the Aubers Ridge. Artillery support was to commence at 06.45 hours, the guns shelling first the positions around Mauquissart and Layes Bridge, and then turning their attention to the road between Pietre and the Bois du Biez. At the same time the German brigades on the Aubers Ridge were to be bombarded by heavy artillery.

Thus at 06.45 hours the British artillery began the scheduled bombardment of the German lines. However, the British commanders were unaware that the Germans had already strengthened their second line and thus the second line was not included in the artillery plan. The attack was therefore beset with problems from the start, as the German artillery launched a three-hour bombardment on the British front lines and assembly areas. Communications also proved a major problem.

The 7th Division began to advance along the Mauquissat road, but the leading 21st Brigade was halted by heavy machine-gun fire. The 8th Division suffered similarly, but managed to capture some farm buildings on the Mauquissart road. At 14.50 hours the Dehra Dun Brigade was ordered to attack the Layes Bridge strongpoint with the 25th Brigade. However, communications again failed, so that the brigades were not assembled in time and the attack was called off; this effectively ended the day's action.

During the night the Germans brought up six battalions to reinforce their line. General Haig had ordered the offensive to be resumed at 10.30 hours the following day, 12 March, but at 04.30 hours the German artillery began shelling the British positions again, especially the rear areas. This was followed by a large German counter-attack at 05.00 hours, involving some 16,000 infantry between Port Arthur and the Moated Grange. This attack was repulsed with heavy German losses. However, the opportunity to advance immediately after the retreating Germans was not followed up, due to the misty weather and the resulting difficulty in registering the artillery. Haig's attack was postponed by two hours. When the artillery finally began shelling the Layes Bridge strongpoint, it made little, if any, impact on the defences and the subsequent attack by the 25th Brigade was driven back with heavy losses. Communications had again failed: the 7th Division, unaware of the postponement, attacked at the original time, but suffered heavy casualties from the machine guns at the Quadrilateral strongpoint. Their attack was called off, leaving several companies stranded without cover.

After accurate shelling by the British artillery, the Quadrilateral was eventually captured, together with 700 prisoners. The British commanders, believing wrongly that the Mauquissart road was occupied by British troops, ordered the 21st Brigade to advance on the Rue d'Enfer. But the Germans still held their position in front of Mauquissart, and the 21st's attack faltered and failed. Communications again were so poor that the staff at the 7th Division headquarters were not aware of the true position until later that evening. Meanwhile the Indian Corps made little progress after reaching the Layes Brook, owing to heavy casualties from machine-gun fire.

The division's advances had by then all been halted, and no further progress was to be made that day. Attempts were made to bring up the 2nd Cavalry Division, but it was too late in the day and too dark. Apart from a futile attack by the 25th Brigade north of the village, the Battle of Neuve Chapelle to all intents and purposes ended in the darkness of 12 March. British casualties numbered about 13,000.

Print No. 235 21 March 1915 Height 6,600ft Scale 1:10000
This shows the main part of the village of Aubers. A probable artillery position is shown at (G).
The dark marks on the print are not cloud shadows, but damage to the glass negative from
chemical splashes.

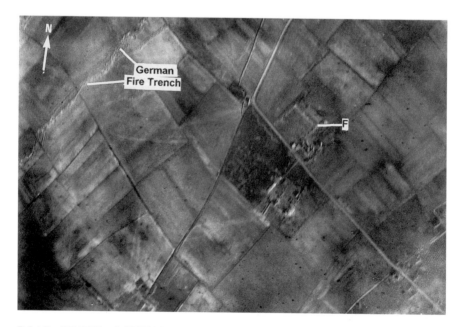

Print No. 236 21 March 1915 Height 5,300ft Scale 1:8000
This print covers the area around Fabrique (F), in the centre of the print. The German trench is
indicated.

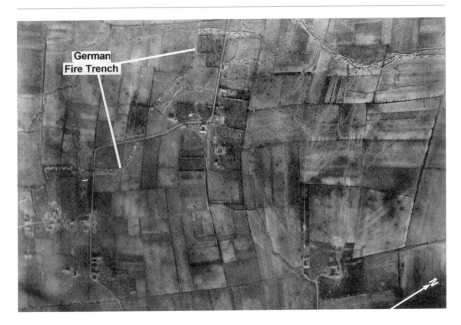

Print No. 239 21 March 1915 Height 6,000ft Scale 1:9100
This shows the German fire trenches on the left of the points reached by the 21st and 24th Brigades on the night of 10/11 March, but from which they were forced to withdraw by German counter-attacks early on the 12th. This fire trench was originally the German second line, and when the photograph was taken on 21 March it did not yet show signs of wire entanglements.

Print No. 242 21 March 1915 Height 6,300ft Scale 1:9500
The photograph covers the German lines between Triveilet and the Rue de Laeval (R).

Print No. 243 21 March 1915 Height 6,000ft Scale: 1:9000
This print shows the German support area between Rue de Laeval (R) to the north and
Aubers (A) in the south. Artillery positions are marked on the map in the vicinity of the print
plot, and a possible battery position is at (G).

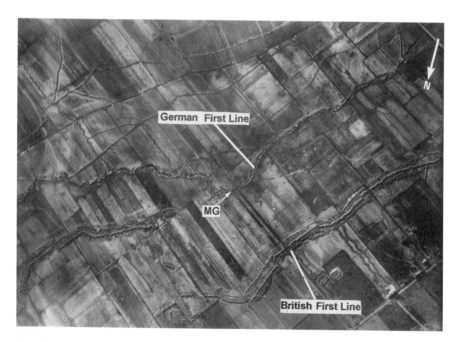

Print No. 245 21 March 1915 Height 5,300ft Scale 1:7900
The area around Le Tilleloy. British and German lines can be seen, with a probable
machine-gun position (MG) marked. The ground is generally wet fields with few shell-holes.

Print No. 456 22 March 1915 Height 8,000ft Scale 1:12000
This shows the assembly area of the Indian Division before the battle. The British front-line trenches lie along the line of the road.

Print No. 253 22 March 1915 Height 8,000ft Scale 1:12000
This shows the main battle area with Neuve Chapelle (arrowed) and the Bois du Biez (B). Lines of trenches can be seen but little further detail. The left side of the print is the approximate position of the 8th Division and the 22nd Brigade.

Print No. 257 22 March 1915 Height 4,400ft Scale 1:6600
The Bois du Biez was reached by the Dehra Dun Brigade of the Indian Corps by 18.30 hours on the first day. The brigade withdrew back across the Layes Brook as German reinforcements entered the wood from the east and launched a counter-attack. The trench lines to the west of the wood are German fire trenches, newly dug after the battle to consolidate the position.

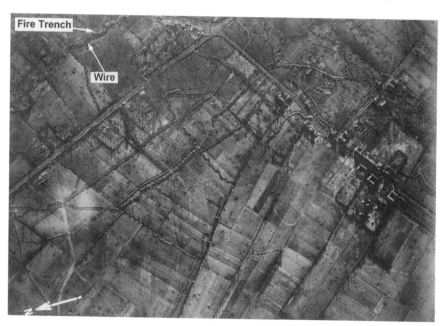

Print No. 260 26 March 1915 Height 4,600ft Scale 1:7000
This shows the position of Port Arthur and its environs. The area at the top of the frame was held by the Garhwal Brigade while the area towards the bottom of the frame was held by the Bareilly Brigade of the Indian Corps. Both British and German trenches can be seen. The German trenches had been captured by this time, but the thin dark line (annotated) in front of the trench indicates the German barbed-wire defences. The thin white line at the back of the fire trench indicates that the trench, having been captured, was being 'reversed' for defence.

Print No. 285 28 March 1915 Height 4,400ft Scale 1:6600
This photograph shows the German front and support line just south of the battle area, with a possible command post at the Farm du Bois (F).

Print No. 302 30 March 1915 Height 6,300ft Scale 1:9500
The German support area near Tourelle. The German support lines lie north of the village, while the distillery is shown at (D).

DESCRIPTION FROM THE AIR PHOTOGRAPHY

While the battlefield was known to be very wet because of the high water table and heavy rains, it is quickly apparent from the photography that the area although shelled is not churned up as in later battles, and all the fields and buildings can be clearly seen. On average, the height at which the photographs were taken has been calculated at around 5,000–6,000ft.

DETAILS OF PHOTOGRAPHS USED

Box	Series	Neg. No.	Date	Map Plot
38	1st Wg	239	21/03/15	36 M 30
38	1st Wg	253	22/03/15	36 M 35
38	1st Wg	456	22/03/15	36 M 33
39	1st Wg	235	21/03/15	36 N 26, 32
39	1st Wg	236	21/03/15	36 N 19
39	1st Wg	237	21/03/15	36 N 9, 15
39	1st Wg	240	21/03/15	36 N 15
39	1st Wg	241	21/03/15	36 N 16
39	1st Wg	242	21/03/15	36 N 14
39	1st Wg	243	21/03/15	36 N 20
39	1st Wg	245	21/03/15	36 N 13
39	1st Wg	254	22/03/15	36 N 31, 32
39	1st Wg	255	22/03/15	36 N 23
39	1st Wg	253	22/03/15	36 N 26
39	1st Wg	256	26/03/15	36 N 27, 28
46	1st Wg	257	22/03/15	36 S 6
46	1st Wg	260	26/03/15	36 S 4
46	1st Wg	285	28/03/15	36 S 16
46	1st Wg	292	29/03/15	36 S 20
46	1st Wg	302	30/03/15	36 S 17

Maps Used

GSGS 3062 1:10000 Sheet 36 SW3 Provisional Edition 24 July 1915
GSGS 3062 1:10000 Sheet 36 SW1 21 July 1915
1st Printing Coy RE GHQ (589b) Map nos 1 and 2 (PRO Ref WO 157 piece no. 127).

LOOS

25–28 SEPTEMBER 1915

Following the Allied Conference, General Joffre decided that there would be an Allied attack in the Arras–Lens and Rheims area. Sir John French agreed with the plan, but voiced reservations following a report from Haig, the Commander of the 1st Army, in which he remarked on the unsuitability of the ground in the Lens–Loos area. Haig concluded that the area was 'for the most part, bare and open … and so swept by rifle and machine-gun fire from German trenches and the numerous fortified villages … that rapid advance would be impossible'.

The assault was to be made on 25 September by divisions of the 1st Army under General Haig on a front of about 4 miles between the town of La Bassée in the north and Lens in the south. The small town of Loos lay just south of the centre of the front, dominated by the winding gear of the mines (known to the British as 'Tower Bridge') and the spoil heap of the Loos Crassier. The German front line was to the west of Givenchy in the north, running southwards, west of Auchy Lez La Bassée via the Hohenzollern Redoubt, the Loos Road Redoubt, Lens Road Redoubt and the Double Crassier west of Loos. Behind the German first line was a second line, which ran from La Bassée in the north via Cite St Elie to Hulluch. At this point the line took the shape of a large D as it looped around to include the village of Cite St Auguste and Cite St Emile.

The First Army consisted of two Corps, the First under General Gough and the Fourth under General Rawlinson, 1 Corps, comprising (from north to south) the 2nd, 9th, and 7th Divisions, held the British left in the north, from Givenchy in the north to the Vermelles–Hulluch road in the south. IV Corps held the British right between the Vermelles–Hulluch Road and the railway to the south of Maroc and Cite St Pierre. It comprised (from north to south) the 1st, 15th, and 47th Divisions, with a mobile reserve known as 'Green Force' based at Le Rutoire. Although not part of Haig's force, XI Corps under General Haking was destined to come under his control; this corps comprised the 21st and 24th Divisions, the first of the 'New Armies' which had arrived in France only a fortnight earlier, and

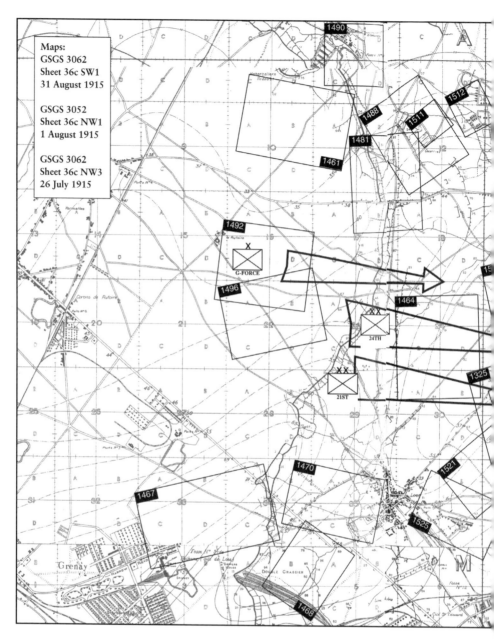

Maps:
GSGS 3062
Sheet 36c SW1
31 August 1915

GSGS 3052
Sheet 36c NW1
1 August 1915

GSGS 3062
Sheet 36c NW3
26 July 1915

had spent three nights moving up to the front line from their concentration area west of St Omer.

The first task set for 1 Corps was to reach the Fosse, Cite St Elie and the northern part of Hulluch. To achieve this, the 2nd Division was to advance along the axis of the Pont Fixe and establish itself along the line of the railway east of Haisnes. The 9th Division was to seize the Hohenzollern Redoubt and drive east

between Douran and Wingles. Meanwhile, the 7th Division was to cross the German front line, secure the quarries and the village of Cite St Elie, and capture Wingles. Once these objectives had been secured, 1 Corps was to drive through the German first and second lines and establish itself on a line through Vedin le Veil, Annay and Loisson. To achieve this, the 1st Division was to take Hulluch itself, while the 15th Division was to take the north side of Loos and the high point known as Hill 70, and then proceed to a point beyond the village of Cite St Auguste. 'Green Force' was to act as a 'flank guard' between the two divisions. Finally the 47th Division on the British far right (to the south) was to secure the Double Crassier and Chalk-pit Copse to secure the Corps flank. The whole assault was to be supported by a four-hour artillery barrage and over 150 tons of chlorine gas.

There were problems from the start. The British artillery barrage proved rather weak, causing little damage to the enemy defences, while the very light and variable wind either failed to carry the gas over the German lines or caused it to linger in front of the British lines. In contrast, the enemy fire was intense and caused high casualties. The First Army divisions enjoyed mixed fortunes. On the British right the 47th Division broke through the German first line in the first hour, suffering about 15 per cent casualties. The left of the division entered the south of Loos and captured Garden City, reaching Chalk-pit Copse by 08.30 hours; however, depleted and under concentrated enfilade fire, the troops could not continue. The troops in the centre and on the right of the 47th Division halted at the German support trench which was then being organised for defence. The 15th Division was seriously hampered by the gas which stayed close to the British line. Nevertheless, their assault took the German trenches, and by 08.00 hours they had captured Loos village despite heavy losses. However, the intensity of the enemy's fire caused the division's frontage to narrow and fragment, so that the extreme left reached the Hulluch–Lens road while the right seized Hill 70, only to be decimated by artillery and machine-gun fire in front of the uncut wire of the German second line. In total, the 15th Division casualties numbered nearly 5,400 men.

The 1st Division attack was badly affected by their own gas and from enfilade fire from the German saps in no-man's-land. The 2nd Brigade on the right suffered over 400 casualties, being stopped in front of the uncut enemy wire. Meanwhile, the 1st Brigade on the left broke through three successive German positions, reaching communication trenches beyond the support line. Elements of the brigade entered Hulluch, but without reinforcements they were forced to withdraw. 'Green Force' was brought up but took heavy casualties and only succeeded in joining the remnants of the 2nd Brigade in front of the uncut wire. Unable to move forward, the British soldiers could either dig in or withdraw under heavy fire as the enemy forces were steadily reinforced. By the end of the first day, the German front line was in British hands, but the second line, although initially breached, had been retaken by German reinforcements and remained intact.

Because of the heavy casualties, Haig sought reinforcements urgently. XI Corps, consisting of the 21st and 24th Divisions, was brought forward during the very wet Saturday night, marching for some eighteen hours. The two divisions formed up along Lone Tree Ridge before advancing to attack the German second line. Artillery support was limited and did not include either divisional or brigade artillery. At 11.00 hours the two divisions advanced in good order into the Loos valley, the 24th Division on the left (to the north), and the 21st on their right (to the south). As the divisions moved into the D-shape of the second German line, they were heavily shelled and machine-gunned from Hulluch on the left and the Bois Hugo on the right, and from the heavily defended line in front of them which was protected by belts of uncut wire. After sustaining over 7,000 casualties, the remnants of the 21st and 24th Divisions returned to positions west of the Lens road until they could be relieved by the Guards Division and withdrawn.

The Guards Division was the last remaining infantry division in the GHQ reserve; their deployment left only the 3rd Cavalry Division in reserve. General Haig sent in the Guards Division initially to hold the line between the Vermelles–Hulluch and the Bethune–Lens roads, relieving the survivors of the 21st and 24th Divisions. On the afternoon of the 27th the 3rd Guards Brigade attacked the Puits 14 bis and the Bois Hugo. While these attacks were pressed with great courage, the artillery and machine-gun fire was so intense that both brigades had to withdraw. Meanwhile the 3rd Cavalry Division, the last reserve, was dismounted and sent to relieve the 15th Division in Loos village.

From the beginning of October, following Marshal Foch's agreement that the French should relieve the British in the Loos village sector, the British First Army, its frontage now greatly reduced, was able to concentrate on its original objective, the Haute Deule canal. The Germans, now reinforced, had recaptured Fosse 8, and fierce fighting had developed around the Hohenzollern Redoubt. An allied attack was proposed by Foch for 3 October, but this had to be postponed because of bad weather. The Germans made a strong counter-attack on 8 October; although this was repulsed it further delayed the First Army's attack until 13 October.

At midday on 13 October, the British First Army began the attack with the objectives of recapturing Fosse 8, and maintaining the line of the Lens–La Bassée road, between the Vermelles–Hulluch road and the chalk pits. A preliminary two-hour artillery bombardment, followed by a gas attack, preceded the assault, but the troops were met with such heavy fire from enemy artillery and entrenched machine guns that they could make no progress.

Further attacks were planned by General Haig for 7 November, but heavy rains and the continuing disruption caused by the German artillery resulted in their abandonment, effectively bringing to an end the Battle of Loos. The total gains of the battle were about 4 miles of German trenches, with a penetration of up to 2 miles. But the cost of this achievement was heavy, with the First Army suffering more than 3,000: the *Official History* states that '800 Officers and 15,000 men were killed, missing or never heard of again'. Total allied losses (French and British) numbered about 115,000, while German losses were estimated at about 50,000.

Print No. 1325 23 September 1915 Height 6,400ft Scale 1:9600
The gun position marked on the map is not confirmed by the photograph. There is a small vehicle/wagon park (W) near Bois Hugo. Communication trenches (C) suggest Bois Hugo is to be occupied and fortified.

Print No. 1332 11 September 1915 Height 5,800ft Scale 1:8800
This area around Cite St Auguste. The photograph shows the German second line with double lines of wire in front of the trench (W), four machine-gun positions (MG), and a heavy trench mortar battery, with six positions (TM).

Print No. 1386 11 September 1915 Height 7,000ft Scale 1:10500
Although of poor quality, this print shows a command post/headquarters area (CP) in the German rear to the east of the Hulluch road.

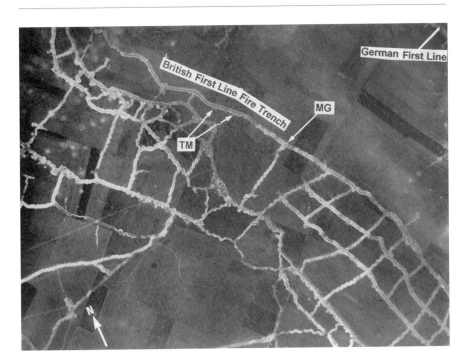

Print No. 1461 22 September 1915 Height 6,000ft Scale 1:9000
British lines in front of the Hohenzollern Redoubt. Trench mortars are shown (TM) plus a machine-gun position (MG).

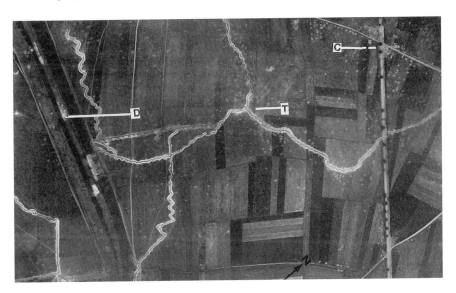

Print No. 1468 23 September 1915 Height 4,600ft Scale 1:7000
This shows the Double Crassier feature (D), to the south-west of Loos, which was attacked and taken by the 47th Division by 09.30 hours on the first day. This photograph was taken two days before the attack and shows the extent of the shelling on the German trenches (T) and the crossroads (C).

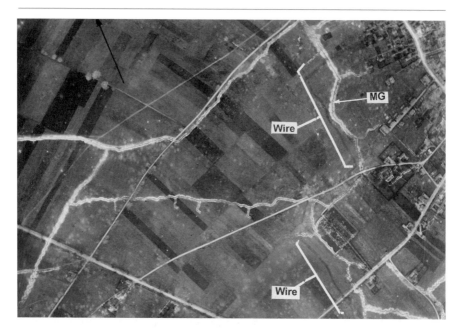

Print No. 1470 23 September 1915 Height 5,250ft Scale 1:8000
This photograph shows a support trench, the front line and the entrenchment around Loos, with wire (W) and machine-gun positions (MG) marked. Also apparent are the effects of shrapnel bursts on the ground.

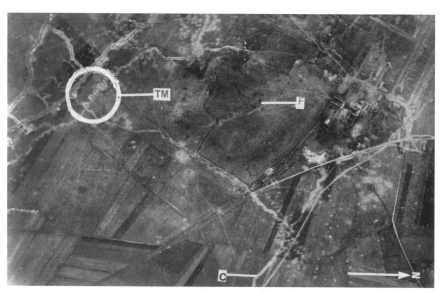

Print No. 1490 23 September 1915 Height 4,600ft Scale 1:6900
The Fosse 8 (F) spoil tip, shown here two days before the assault by the 28th Brigade. They took Fosse 8, reaching the Corons Trench (C) to the east. However, by 28 September the Germans, considerably reinforced, had succeeded in recapturing the position. On 13 October another British effort to retake Fosse 8 failed under heavy artillery and machine-gun fire. A trench mortar battery is shown (TM).

Print No. 1512 11 September 1915 Height 3,000ft Scale 1:4400
This shows the second line around Cite St Elie. Note the double wire around the village. Trench mortar (TM), and machine-gun (MG) positions are marked. There are dugouts in the front line.

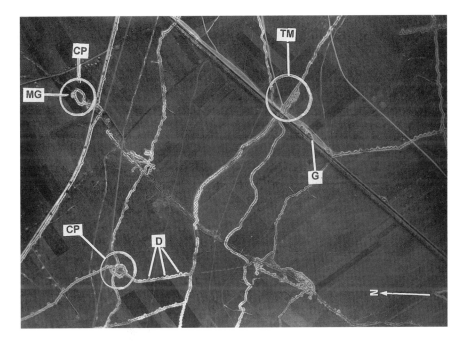

Print No. 1464 23 September 1915 Height 5,600ft Scale 1:8400
Communication trenches. Indicated are a probable command post (CP), a probable trench mortar (TM), a possible gun position (G), dugouts (D), and a strong point (SP) with a possible machine gun (MG).

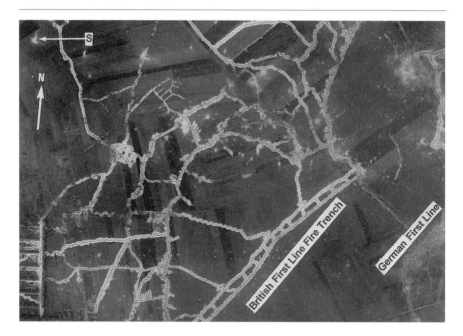

Print No. 1467 23 September 1915 Height 5,300ft Scale 1:7900
The British and German lines immediately in front of Loos, photographed two days before the attack. A possible shell-burst is marked (S).

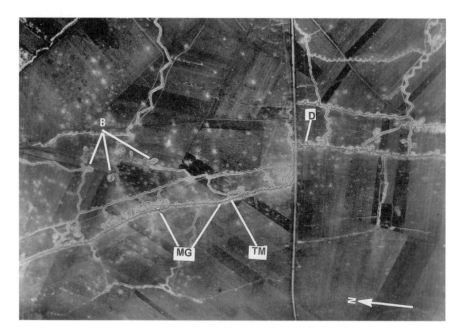

Print No. 1481 23 September 1915 Height 5,000ft Scale 1:7400
The German front line across the main road. New bunker/shelters (B) are under construction. Machine gun (MG), trench mortar positions (TM), and dugouts (D) are visible in the support line.

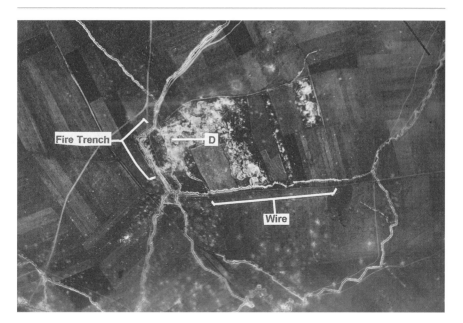

Print No. 1488 23 September 1915 Height 5200ft Scale 1:7800
On the left of this photograph can be seen the fire trench defending the second line around the quarries. There is a dugout (D) in the quarries, and wire defences on the west.

Print No. 1492 24 September 1915 Height 5,200ft Scale 1:7800
This photograph shows the British front-line and support trenches. Note the command post (CP) known as 'Daly's Keep'. These trenches in front of Le Rutoire Farm were occupied by the 3rd Brigade and 'Green Force'.

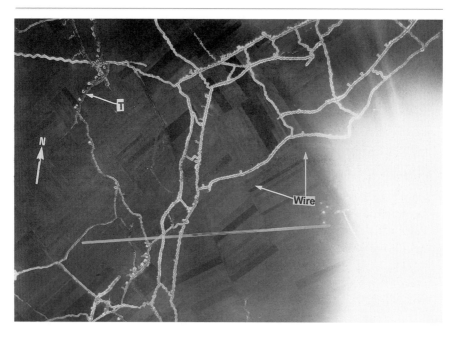

Print No. 1496 24 September 1915 Height 5,300ft Scale 1:7900
The British lines the day before the attack. This photograph was taken in the early morning into the sun, hence the 'sun-burst' exposure. This damaged print shows the British wire and some flooded and abandoned trenches (T).

Print No. 1511 26 September 1915 Height 2,000ft Scale 1:3000
This shows the quarries which were fiercely fought over by the 22nd Brigade of the 7th Division.

Print No. 1531 26 September 1915 Height 4,000ft Scale 1:6000
This photograph was taken just after midday and there is no military activity to be seen. Comparison with Print No. 1332 shows no change, indicating that the attack by the 21st and 24th Divisions had not yet reached this point.

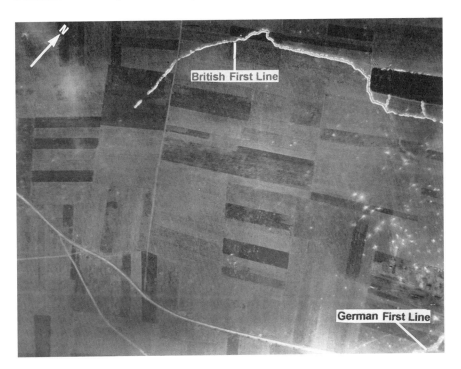

Print No. 1521 28 September 1915 Height 4,300ft Scale 1:6500
This covers the area of the wood to the west of the Bois Hugo with new British trenches and the results of shelling around the German trenches.

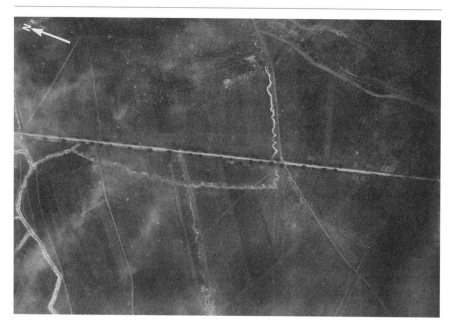

Print No. 1523 28 September 1915 Height 3,600ft Scale 1:5500
German fire trenches and communication trenches south of Hulluch, which enfiladed the
advance of the 24th Division two days earlier.

Print No. 1525 28 September 1915 Height 4,600ft Scale 1:7000
The slag heap on the east side of Loos, showing a newly constructed fire trench which is
probably British.

Print No. 1524 29 September 1915 Height 5,300ft Scale 1:7900

This photograph was taken after the battle and shows communication trenches leading into Bois Hugo, suggesting that the wood is defended. Apparent ground damage from muzzle-blast suggests a possible former gun position (G). New trenches, probable digging-in scrapes (S), appear to be unoccupied.

DESCRIPTION FROM THE AIR PHOTOGRAPHY

The quality of the photography is considerably better than that taken six months earlier at Neuve Chapelle. The trenches appear to be in good condition, and the ground appears relatively dry with few shell-holes among the fields.

DETAILS OF PHOTOGRAPHS USED

Box	Series	Neg. No.	Date	Map Plot
60	1st Wg	1461	22/09/15	36c G 4, 10
60	1st Wg	1464	23/09/15	36c G 17, 18, 23
60	1st Wg	1467	23/09/15	36c G 27, 28, 32
60	1st Wg	1470	23/09/15	36c G 28, 27, 34
60	1st Wg	1481	23/09/15	36c G 11
60	1st Wg	1488	23/09/15	36c G 6, 12
60	1st Wg	1490	23/09/15	36c G5
60	1st Wg	1492	24/09/15	36c G 15, 16, 21
60	1st Wg	1496	24/09/15	36c G 16, 17, 22
61	1st Wg	1511	26/09/15	36c G 6a
61	1st Wg	1521	28/09/15	36c G 30
61	1st Wg	1525	28/09/15	36c G 36
62	1st Wg	1322	11/09/15	36c H 19
62	1st Wg	1332	11/09/15	36c H 32
62	1st Wg	1386	11/09/15	36c H 21
62	1st Wg	1523	28/09/15	36c H 25
62	1st Wg	1524	29/09/15	36c H 31
65	1st Wg	1513	26/09/15	36c G 12
65	1st Wg	1515	26/09/15	36c G 6
66	1st Wg	1468	23/09/15	36c M4
66	1st Wg	1512	11/09/15	36c G6
66	1st Wg	1325	23/09/15	36c H25
66	1st Wg	1531	26/09/15	36c H13

Maps Used
GSGS 3062 1:10000 Sheet 36c NW3 Edition A 26 July 1915
GSGS 3062 1:10000 France Provisional Edition Sheet 36c SW1 31 August 1915
GSGS 3052 1:10000 France Provisional Edition Sheet 36c NW1 1 August 1915

THE SOMME – LA BOISSELLE

1–7 JULY 1916

The front for the first day of the Somme battle covered more than 20 miles. This study is restricted to the area of La Boisselle.

> The whole section of our front, from Thiepval, down past Boisselle, round the Fricourt salient, and on to Montauban, was to be photographed every day, in order that Headquarters might have accurate information of the effects of the bombardment. This aimed at destroying all the enemy first- and second-line trenches, and so making the attack easy for the infantry.
>
> At leisure we had photographed the line before the bombardment started. But during this last week the weather was poor. On two days, low clouds and rain prevented us getting any photos at all. The 3rd and 15th Corps, for whom we were working, got in a panic. It was essential to know the effect of the shelling. Photos were to be got at all costs …
>
> Clouds forced us down to two thousand feet … At two thousand feet we were in the path of the gun trajectories, and as the shells passed above or below us, the wind eddies made by their motion flung the machine up and down as if in a gale. Each bump meant that a passing shell had missed the machine by four or five feet.

★ Extract from *Sagittarius Rising*, Cecil Lewis, 1936.

In June 1916, III Corps, consisting of the 8th and 34th Divisions, covered a front of about 2½ miles to the north-east of Albert astride the old Roman road from Albert to Bapaume. The 8th Division was positioned north of the road facing Ovillers and Pozières, on the Corps boundary with X Corps and flanked to the north by the 32nd Division. To the south of the Roman road, the 34th Division faced Contalmaison, Sausage Valley and Mametz Wood. The 8th Division, led by

Maj. Gen. Hudson, was ordered to capture the villages of Ovillers and Pozières. This required an ascent up the Ovillers spur before advancing to Pozières, 2,000yds further on. Hudson protested that the divisional frontage was excessive and that his men would be subject to enfilade fire from the Thiepval spur on the division's left flank, and from La Boisselle on the right, but his objections were overruled by General Rawlinson.

After a week of heavy artillery bombardment, at 07.30 hours on 1 July the whistles were blown and a general advance was made 'over the top'.

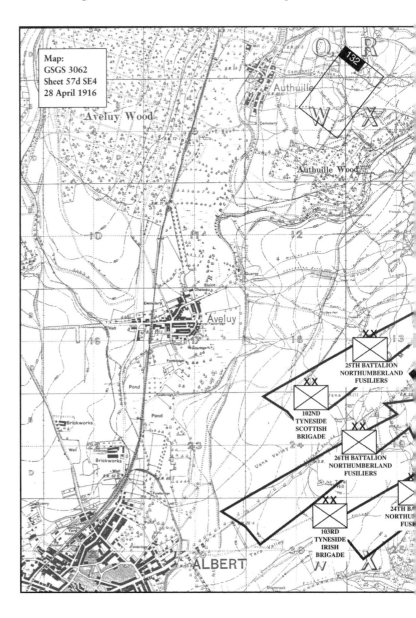

Map:
GSGS 3062
Sheet 57d SE4
28 April 1916

25TH BATTALION
NORTHUMBERLAND
FUSILIERS

102ND
TYNESIDE
SCOTTISH
BRIGADE

26TH BATTALION
NORTHUMBERLAND
FUSILIERS

24TH B.
NORTHU
FUS

103RD
TYNESIDE
IRISH
BRIGADE

The 8th Division, consisting of the 20th, 23rd and 25th Brigades, advanced in good order in extended lines until the first line was about 100yds from the German wire. At this point the enemy opened fire with machine guns, rifles, mortars and artillery into the dense mass of advancing infantry. In addition, as had been predicted by Maj. Gen. Hudson, his men suffered intense enfilade fire from both the Thiepval spur and the enemy positions at La Boisselle. Nevertheless, the division penetrated the German lines to a depth of about 500yds on the left and about 100yds on the right. However, casualties were so

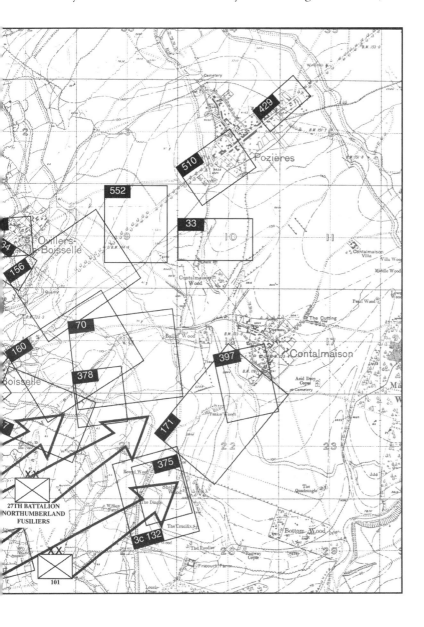

high that only a few men reached these points and were quickly driven back by local counter-attacks.

Of the division's brigades engaged in the fighting, the casualties were as follows: 20th Brigade: 1,196, 23rd Brigade: 1,502 and 25th Brigade: 1,410. The 34th Division, under Maj. Gen. Ingouville-Williams, faced the village of La Boisselle, with valleys on either side. Mash Valley was to the north of the village and Sausage Valley to the south. In preparation for the attack, two mines had been laid on either side of La Boisselle: one at Y Sap to the north, next to the road, and the other at Lochnagar to the south-east of the village. The mine in Y Sap was charged with 46,000lb of ammonal; that at Lochnagar contained 60,000lb of ammonal; both were timed to explode at 07.25 hours.

Astride the Albert–Bapaume road, facing Mash Valley, was the 102nd Tyneside Scottish Brigade, comprising the 20th, 21st, 24th and 23rd Northumberland Fusiliers (known as the 1st, 2nd, 3rd and 4th Tyneside Scottish respectively). To their right was the 101st Brigade, comprising the 10th Lincolns, 11th Suffolks, and the 15th and 16th Royal Scots. In support a mile to the rear on the Tara–Usna line was the 103rd Tyneside Irish Brigade, comprising the 24th, 25th, 26th and 27th Brigades Northumberland Fusiliers (known respectively as the 1st, 2nd, 3rd and 4th Tyneside Irish).

When the mines exploded, the strongpoints that they had been designed to destroy were successfully put out of action. The 102nd Tyneside Scottish Brigade began its advance to the sound of bagpipes. In eight successive waves, the men walked in straight lines to cover the half-mile to the German wire. As the 102nd and the 101st Brigades advanced respectively into Mash and Sausage Valleys, they were exposed to heavy enfilade fire from the La Boisselle spur. Despite the continuous heavy shelling over the preceding week, the German defenders and their guns had survived in the deep shelters, and were now presented with such easy targets they couldn't miss.

The brigades advanced into a storm of machine-gun and rifle fire, as well as artillery shells. Within minutes the brigades in the valleys on either side of La Boisselle were destroyed. Only on the far right, away from the La Boisselle spur, did a few British troops gain the edge of the Lochnagar mine crater, while further on a small group penetrated the German line and captured a small redoubt 700yds beyond. No progress at all was made in front of La Boisselle.

Meanwhile, the 103rd Tyneside Irish Brigade had begun their advance from the Tara–Usna line a mile to the rear. As they advanced down the slope and across the valley floor they also came under heavy fire and lost men in large numbers all the way. On the left they were stopped before La Boisselle, but on the right they managed to continue and pressed on into the German lines. However, the casualties had been so great that of the 2,500 men of the brigade who had started the attack, fewer than fifty were still capable of fighting. Of the 6,392 men of the 34th Division, 1,927 were killed on this day.

At the end of the day only the Royal Scots, on the extreme right, had managed to penetrate the German lines, advancing to a depth of about half a mile. The German line immediately in front of the Lochnagar crater had been captured, but the rest of the German line remained intact. There were no other British gains at all.

Plans for a night attack by 19th Division on La Boisselle, intended to take place at 22.30 hours on 1 July, came to nothing. The congestion in the forward area had prevented the 57th and 58th Brigades from getting into position and it was not until dawn on 2 July that elements of the 58th Brigade relieved part of the 34th Division at the Schwaben Hohen (crater). The 58th Brigade, together with the 34th Division, was then detailed to attack at 16.00 hours the Sausage Redoubt and the trenches beyond, on a front of about 1,000yds. After half an hour's artillery bombardment of Ovillers, the 58th Brigade attacked under cover of a smokescreen. The German line west of La Boisselle was captured with relatively few casualties and the western part of the village was successfully cleared by 21.00 hours. At the end of the day, the line was consolidated along the road, stopping short of the church.

On 3 July the 34th Division attempted to link up with the 19th Division, but its three bombing attacks failed, and the men were relieved by the 23rd Division at the end of the day. Meanwhile, the 57th and 58th Brigades of the 19th Division led an attack at 14.15 hours on the German lines between La Boisselle and the Albert road. An hour later, both brigades attacked La Boisselle itself, taking most of the village, and continued onwards, capturing the German trenches 400yds further on beyond the village. Despite heavy German bombardment and counter-attacks, the brigades gained the eastern end of the village, although the Germans still held a line running to the church.

The following day, the 19th Division attacked the remaining Germans in La Boisselle with strong support from Stokes mortars and machine guns. The attack started at 08.30 hours and after heavy fighting the Germans were cleared from the village.

On 5 July the 19th Division attempted to clear the enemy re-entrant on the east side of the village, but it was not until the following day that the position was taken by a direct assault over open ground. Once in position, the division then repulsed three German counter-attacks.

Beyond La Boisselle, on the north-east side, was a strong German trench, with another one running south-west from Bailiff Wood. This was the objective of the 19th Division on 7 July. The attack by the 56th and 58th Brigades began at 08.15 hours, behind an artillery barrage. The objective was captured and the position consolidated.

Print No. 33 1 July 1916 Height 3,600ft Scale 1:5500
This photograph shows the defences between Contalmaison Wood and Pozières. The circled area apparently contains four newly prepared covered positions, possibly large trench mortars (TM).

Print No. 171 1 July 1916 Height 5,400ft Scale 1:8100
The considerable tracking on this photograph indicates recent transport movements.

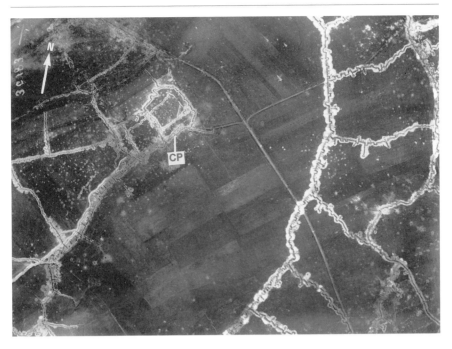

Print No. 183 1 July 1916 Height 3,000ft Scale 1:4500
The area of 101 Brigade in the rear of the British lines on the east side of Becourt. Note the probable HQ (CP).

Print No. 510 16 July 1916 Height 3,400ft Scale 1:5000
The print shows the area around the village of Pozières.

Print No. 4c 132 16/05 July 1916 Height 3,600ft Scale: 1:4500
This photograph was probably taken in June 1916 before the main preliminary bombardment. The British and German lines are very close at this point. A probable machine gun (MG) is indicated.

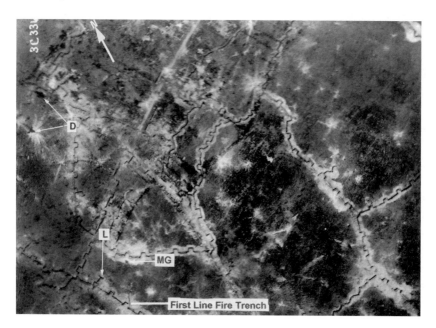

Print No. 334 1–6 July 1916 (probably) Height 2,400ft Scale 1:3600
This photograph shows the southern edge of Ovillers La Boisselle. The front-line firing trench is marked, with a probable machine-gun position (MG) and a latrine (L). (D) indicates the position of dugouts.

Print No. 347 1–6 July 1916 (probably) Height 4,400ft Scale 1:6600
The large crater (C) at the bottom is probably Lochnagar. Probable dugouts are indicated at (D) while a probable machine-gun position is at (MG).

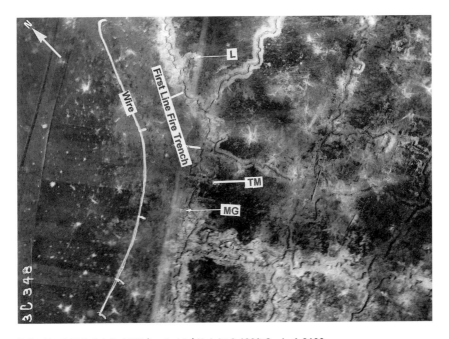

Print No. 348 1–6 July 1916 (probably) Height 2,400ft Scale 1:3600
Part of the area around Ovillers La Boisselle, facing Mash Valley. The front-line fire trench and part of the wire defences are marked. Probable trench mortars (TM) and machine guns (MG) are also indicated.

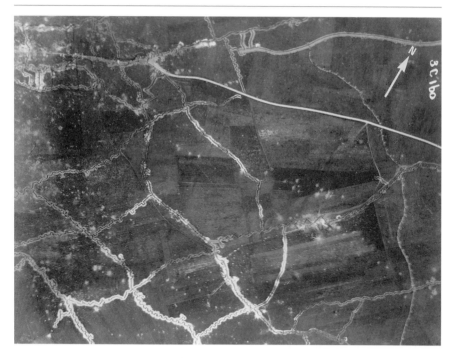

Prints Nos 160 and 70 1–6 July 1916 (probably) Height 4,800ft Scale 1:7200
These photographs show Sausage Valley. It is apparent that despite the devastation around no-man's-land, Sausage Valley remains largely fields interspersed with trenches.

Print No. 3c 132 1 July 1916 (probably) Height 4,000ft Scale 1:6000

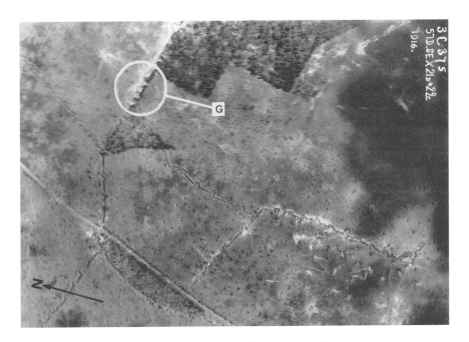

Print No. 375 1–6 July 1916 (probably) Height 1,100ft Scale 1:5000
Round Wood, Birch Tree Wood and Shelter Wood. These photographs were taken at different times and make an interesting comparison. The top picture was taken perhaps late in June, while the lower picture was probably taken a few weeks later when the tree foliage had been considerably reduced, probably by shellfire. Area G contains a possible artillery position.

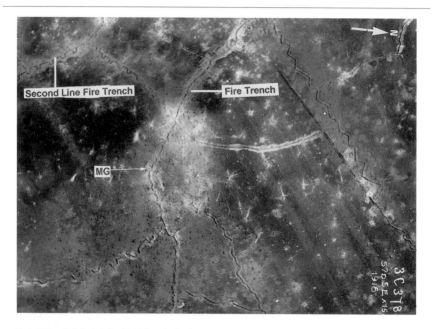

Print No. 378 1–6 July 1916 (probably) Height 2,800ft Scale 1:4200
The north end of Sausage Valley. The German second-line firing trench is marked, as is the third-line firing trench. A possible machine-gun position (MG) is also marked.

Print No. 415 6 July 1916 Height 1,500ft Scale 1:2200
This shows the Y Sap crater (C) on the north side of La Boisselle, on the edge of Mash Valley. The crater was over 110ft across. While the mine may have destroyed a sap trench, it appears to have had little effect on the main firing trench. The front trenches have been heavily bombarded but they appear to have suffered relatively little damage, with trench covers and crossing points still in place. The dark spots marked (D) indicate dugout entrances.

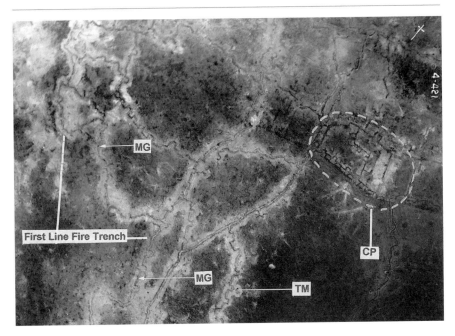

Print No. 421 6 July 1916 Height 1,900ft Scale 1:2700
This photograph shows the edge of the village and Sausage Valley, and includes destroyed buildings. The front line has been heavily shelled. (MG) indicates probable machine-gun positions while TM is a probable trench mortar site. (CP) indicates a strongpoint/HQ area.

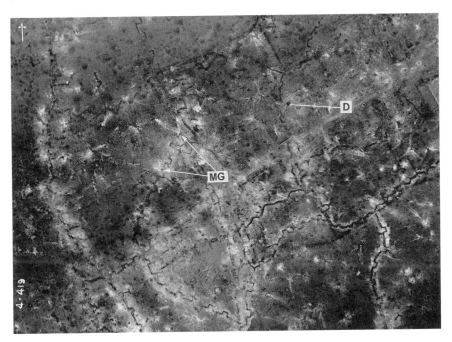

Print No. 419 6 July 1916 Height 2,300ft Scale 1:3300
(D) marks a deep dugout entrance. (MG) indicates probable machine-gun positions.

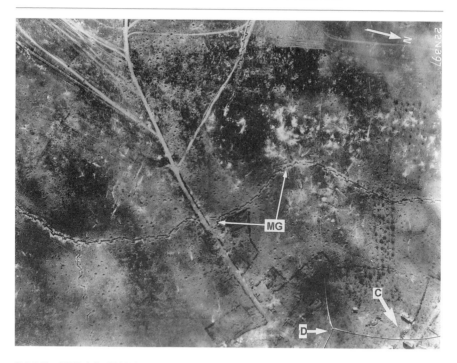

Print No. 397 8 July 1916 Height 3,000ft Scale 1:4500
The edge of Contalmaison village (C), with the German defences in front. (MG) indicates a probable machine-gun position. (D) indicates a crack in the glass negative.

Print No. 429 9 July 1916 Height 2,700ft Scale 1:3900
The edge of the village of Pozières, showing some trenches around the village.

Print No. 156 1 July 1916 Height 5,300ft Scale 1:7900

Running across the centre of this picture is the road from Albert, with the light railway (RLY) to the south running almost parallel to the road.

Print No. 552 20 July 1916 Height 3,600ft Scale 1:5400

This covers the road to the south-west of Pozières along which the Australians advanced. The photograph was taken about midday, hence the position of the 'sun-burst' of over-exposure on the edge of the print. A German support trench is visible along the edge of the road.

DESCRIPTION FROM THE AIR PHOTOGRAPHY

The area is seen to be chalky and was apparently dry and devoid of mud. The effects of the seven-day artillery barrage are clearly visible around the front-line trenches, which remain in surprisingly good condition. From the archive data, it is apparent that photographs taken during the crucial period between 1 and 6 July were not properly logged and catalogued at the time, so that a considerable number of prints which were obviously taken in July are dated merely as '1916'. As other prints are precisely dated before and after this period, it is probably safe to assume that those dated only 1916 were taken during this period.

DETAILS OF PHOTOGRAPHS USED

Box	Series	Neg. No.	Date	Map Plot
251a	3c	334	01/07/16	57d X 8
251a	3c	347	01/07/16	57d X 14, 20
251a	3c	348	01/07/16	57d X 13, 14
251A	3c	375	01/07/16	57d X 21, 22
251A	3c	378	01/07/16	57d X 15c
249	4c	132	16/05/16	57d X 1 R 31
249	4c	415	06/07/16	57d X 14
249	4c	419	06/07/16	57d X 8
249	4c	421	06/07/16	57d X 14, 20
249	4c	429	09/07/16	57d X 4
249	4c	510	16/07/16	57d X 3, 4
249	4c	552	20/07/16	57d X 9
250	22n	397	08/07/16	57d X 16
251	3c	33	01/07/16	57d X 10
251	3c	70	01/07/16	57d X 15
251	3c	132	01/07/16	57d X 21, 22, 27
251	3c	156	01/07/16	57d X 8, 9, 14
251	3c	160	01/07/16	57d X 14, 15
251	3c	171	01/07/16	57d X 16, 22
251	3c	183	01/07/16	57d X 26

Maps Used
GSGS 3062 1:10000 Ovillers Sheet 57d SE4 Edition 2B 28 April 1916

FLERS-COURCELETTE

15–23 SEPTEMBER 1916

The Flers–Courcelette battle marked the start of the second phase of the 1916 Somme offensive, and is remembered principally for the first use of tanks in battle. The attack was to be made across the front of the Reserve and Fourth Armies, with the objective of seizing Martinpuich and Courcelette on the first day. The troops allocated for the attack were as follows. On the British left was the 15th Scottish Division in front of Martinpuich, with the 50th Northumberland Division on their right. To their right (but below High Wood) was the 47th London Division. The centre of XV Corps was at Delville Wood, on the north side of which was the 41st Division. On its left was the New Zealand Division, while the 14th Division was on the right of the 41st. The XV Corps consisted of the 56th London Division, the Guards Division and the 6th Division. The ground for the assault was covered from left to right by the Reserve Army and the Fourth Army, with the French on the extreme right. The Fourth Army extended between the Combles Ravine and Martinpuich, with III Corps on the left, XV Corps in the centre and XIV Corps on the right.

The Fourth Army was to be the main attack force. Its objective was to break through the enemy's defensive line and occupy Flers, Gueudecourt and Morval-Lesboeufs. The breakthrough would be followed up by the Cavalry Corps which was to gallop through the breach and seize the high ground about Sufles Villers, Rocquigny Reincourt, Les Bapaume and Bapaume. To help achieve the breakthrough, tanks were to be used for the first time: seventeen were allotted to XIV Corps and another seventeen to XV Corps, with a further eight to III Corps and seven to the Reserve Army.

Following a three-day artillery bombardment, the attack began at 06.20 hours on 15 September. Although the tanks were few in number, the effect of those leading the XV Corps attack was sensational. Nine tanks moved forward with the leading infantry while nine more 'mopped-up' behind. In a little over three hours, the left-hand division of XV Corps followed a solitary tank up the main street of Flers and through the German third line. On the right, things did not go so well. On the right of the 14th Division was the Guards Division, with the 6th Division on their right attacking the Quadrilateral.

The 1st and 2nd Guards Brigades did not in the event get the ten tanks allocated to them, while the five tanks that reached the start line all became unserviceable or lost direction. However, without the tanks and despite heavy losses, the Guards took and held the Triangle strongpoint 500yds north of the Quadrilateral. To the north of Delville Wood the 14th Division, with the aid of a single tank, overcame the German first line and reached the second line. At the same time as the 41st Division attacked towards Flers, the New Zealand Division on the left captured the trench facing them, and then took the German

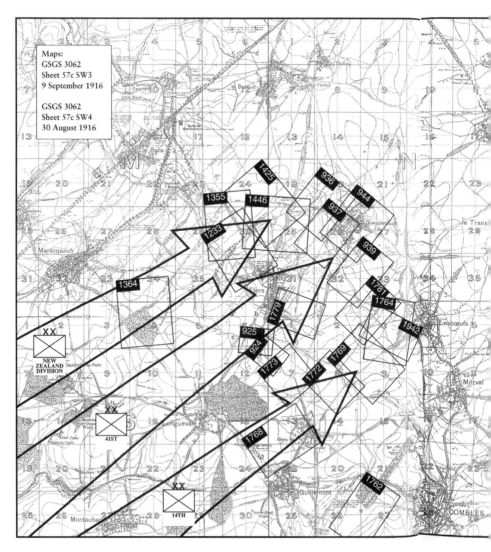

positions to the north and north-west of Flers. The 50th Division then took the position to the west of High Wood. With both flanks of High Wood taken, the 47th London Division was able to capture the wood itself, although they suffered heavy casualties.

At Martinpuich and north of the Albert–Bapaume road, the 2nd and 3rd Canadian Divisions outran their tank support and headed for Courcelette.

The 41st Division, between Delville Wood and High Wood, had the support of seven of the ten allocated tanks and quickly advanced in front of the tanks to take the first line of German trench. The infantry then followed the tanks through the second line and by noon a single tank was in the high street in Flers.

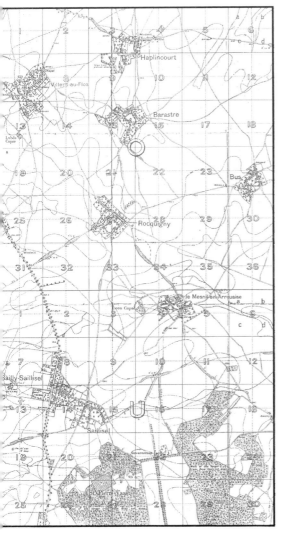

Despite high casualties, the overall advance, aided by the tanks, had covered more than 2,000yds, but German reinforcements prevented the hoped-for breakthrough.

The day began with sunny weather. In the XIV Corps area, the Guards Division began an advance at about 07.30 hours and captured the section of the Ginchy–Lesboeufs road that had been their objective the previous day. Later at 13.30 hours the 3rd Guards Brigade advanced without artillery support and came under such heavy machine-gun fire that they were forced to dig in about 250yds short of their objective. They were later relieved by the 20th Division during the night, in heavy rain.

At the same time, XV Corps launched an attack along the whole of its front. The 14th Division moved forwards under a weak artillery barrage, but under sustained machine-gun fire the men soon faltered; although it was restarted at 19.00 hours, the attack failed.

The 41st Division attack was led by the 64th Brigade. Although late in starting off behind the barrage, and suffering considerably from machine-gun and shellfire, the brigade managed to advance 1,300yds, but could not reach Grid Trench, the objective. A supporting tank continued on to Gueudecourt, but was destroyed by artillery, and the attack could not be restarted before nightfall. Earlier in the day, the New Zealand Division, with the help of a tank, had stopped a German advance down the Ligny road. The leading brigade had attacked at 09.00 hours and secured a sector of Grove Valley, but further advances were impossible.

Heavy rain now set in. On the 17th, the 20th Division drove off a German attack but the division's counter-attack gained no ground. In the XV Corps area, the 14th Division was relieved by the 21st and the 41st by the 55th Division. Heavy and almost continuous rain turned the ground into a quagmire of deep mud so that further assaults were impossible, and the action of Flers–Courcelette was effectively closed down.

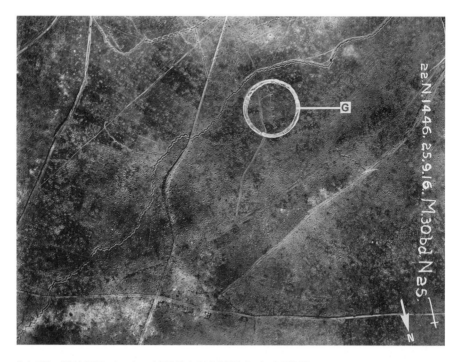

Print No. 1446 25 September 1916 Height 6,800ft Scale 1:10300
Factory Corner, showing the communication trenches supporting the German second line. A line of four possible field-gun positions are indicated at [G].

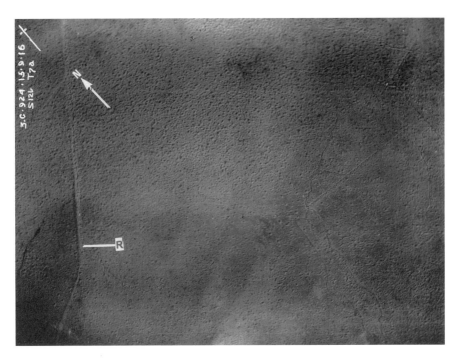

Print Nos 924 and 925 15 September 1916 Height 4,000ft Scale 1:6000
These prints show the heavily shelled area to the north of Delville Wood. The only feature of
any note is the sunken road (R) from Longueval to Flers.

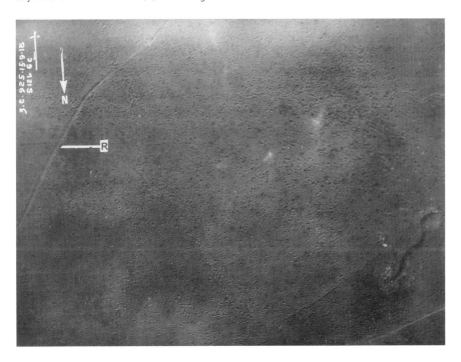

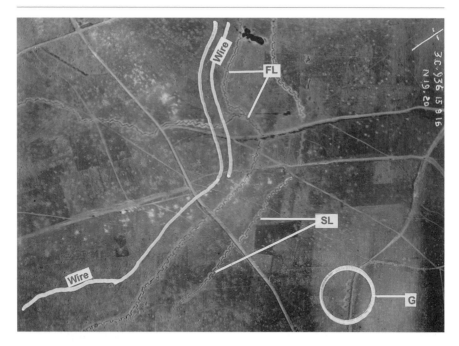

Print No. 936 15 September 1916 Height 6,000ft Scale 1:9100
This photograph shows the German second line. The firing line (FL) and the support line (SL) are marked, while (G) indicates a probable field-gun battery position. Wire can also be seen.

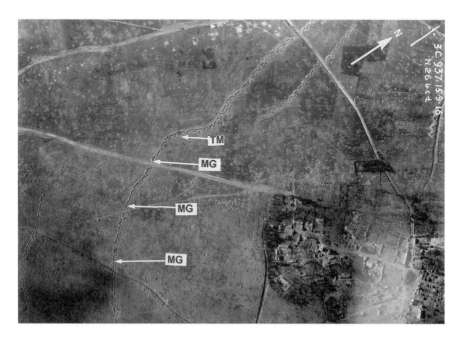

Print No. 937 15 September 1916 Height 6,400ft Scale 1:9600
The German second line near the village of Gueudecourt. Probable machine guns (MG) and a trench mortar position (TM) are marked. Most of the village is ruined, the houses roofless.

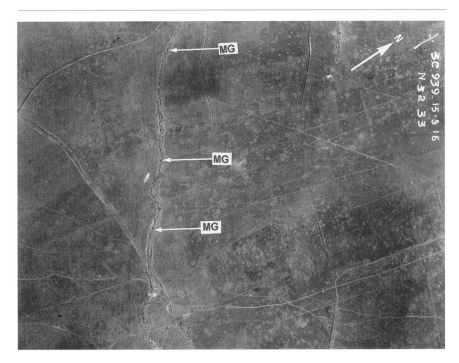

Print No. 939 15 September 1916 Height 6,000ft Scale 1:9200
The German second line south of Gueudecourt. Probable machine-gun positions are marked.

Print No. 944 15 September 1916 Height 6,600ft Scale 1:10000
The ruins of Gueudecourt. A probable field-gun position is marked (G).

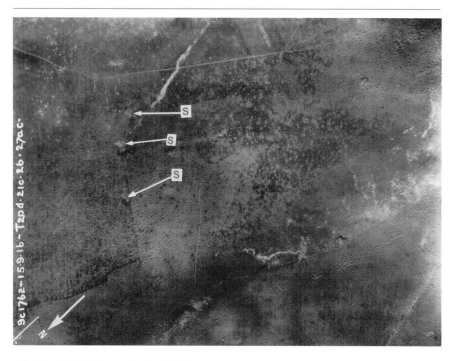

Print No. 1762 15 September 1916 Height 6,800ft Scale 1:110300
Leuze Wood, east of Guillemont. Shell-bursts are marked [S].

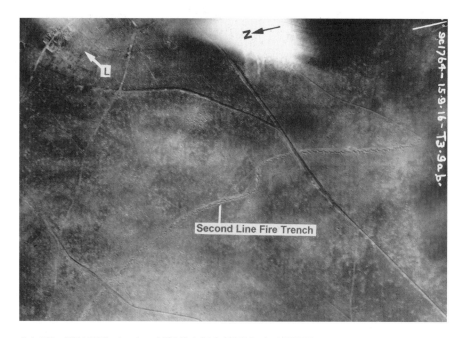

Print No. 1764 15 September 1916 Height 6,600ft Scale 1:10000
This shows the German second-line trench, which crosses the road from Lesboeufs (L), on the day of the attack. The ruins of the village can be seen in the corner of the print.

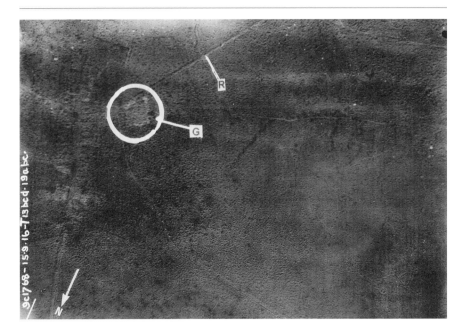

Print No. 1768 15 September 1916 Height 6,600ft Scale 1:10000
This print shows the total devastation of Ginchy: it has been reduced entirely to rubble and marks in the mud. The road to Guillemont (R) is at the top of the print. Virtually nothing remains of Ginchy Farm (G) near the village crossroads.

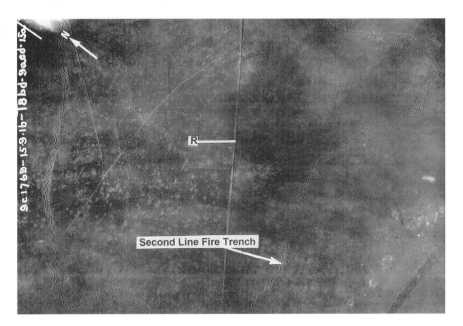

Print No. 1769 15 September 1916 Height 6,600ft Scale 1:10000
This shows the continuation of the road (R) from Print 1764. The trenches are difficult to see but are the main fire trenches of the German second line. The Ginchy–Lesboeufs road (R) runs across the centre of the print.

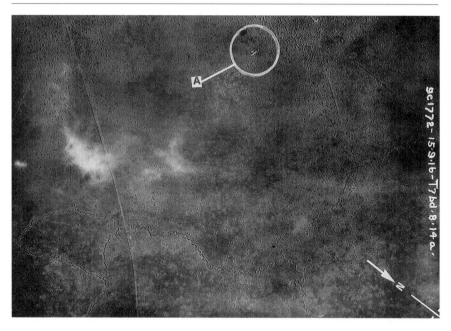

Print No. 1772 15 September 1916 Height 6,400ft Scale 1:9600
The German front line and the Ginchy–Lesboeufs road. The aircraft (A) has been identified as an FE2b going out on patrol over enemy lines.

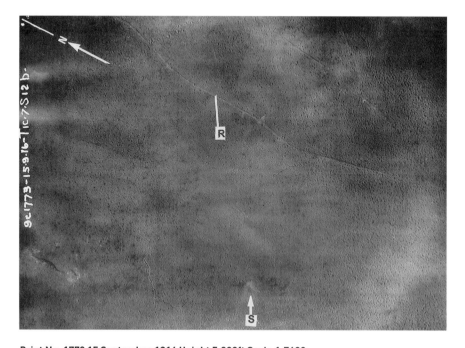

Print No. 1773 15 September 1916 Height 5,000ft Scale 1:7600
This featureless area of mud and shell-holes lies immediately north-east of Delville Wood. The Flers–Ginchy road (R) runs diagonally across the print. A shell-burst is shown at (S).

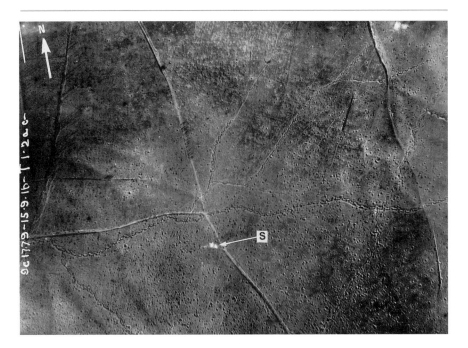

Print No. 1779 15 September 1916 Height 4,800ft Scale 1:7200
Area on the eastern edge of Flers. Note the shell-burst at (S).

Print No. 1781 15 September 1916 Height 6,000ft Scale 1:9000
This print covers the German second-line trenches between Gueudecourt and Lesboeufs. A shell-burst (S) can be seen near the road. The presence of wire is indicated by the dark tone.

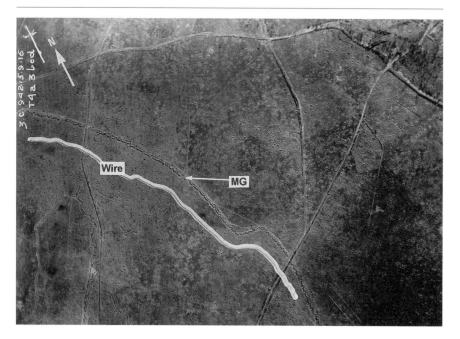

Print No. 1942 15 September 1916 Height 5,800ft Scale 1:8800
The German second line near Lesboeufs. There is a possible machine-gun position (MG), and wire belts are marked.

Print No. 1355 22 September 1916 Height 6,600ft Scale 1:10000
This print shows the area between Le Sars and Flers which has been heavily shelled. A German communication trench (C) is marked where it crosses the road cutting.

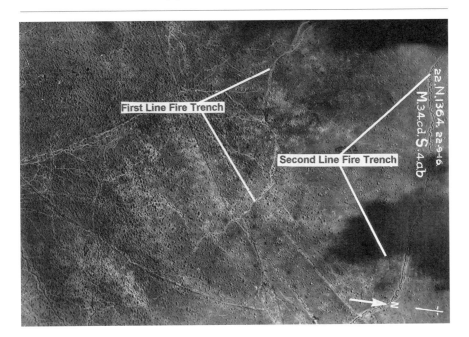

First Line Fire Trench

Second Line Fire Trench

22.N.1364. 22-9-16.
M.34.cd.S.4.ab

Print No. 1364 22 September 1916 Height 6,800ft Scale 1:10300
High Wood. This area was the scene of hard fighting. The German front line is not built to textbook pattern, probably owing to the original density of the wood. When this photograph was taken, the wood had lost all its foliage and most of its trees, leaving open, unprotected and heavily shelled ground for the British attack.

22.N.1425. 23-9-16.M.24 bcd.,19ac.30b.
N.25a.

Print No. 1425 23 September 1916 Height 6,800ft Scale 1:10300
The German third-line defences at Factory Corner. The area consisted mainly of open fields with few defences and had been heavily shelled.

DESCRIPTION FROM THE AIR PHOTOGRAPHY

The very wet nature of the ground, and the effects of prolonged and intense shelling which turned the ground into a morass, can be quickly appreciated from the photography. The obliteration of landmarks made the work of target location very difficult for the photographic interpreters, and their results in plotting and interpreting prints show how skilled they were.

DETAILS OF PHOTOGRAPHS USED

Box	Series	Neg. No.	Date	Map Plot
155	22N	1233	09/09/16	57c M 29, 30, 36
155	22N	1355	22/09/16	57c M 29, 30
155	22N	1364	22/09/16	57c M 34, S 4
155	22N	1425	23/09/16	57c M 24, N 19
155	22N	1446	25/09/16	57c 30 N 25
169	3c	936	15/09/16	57c N 19, 20
169	3c	937	15/09/16	57c N 26
169	3c	939	15/09/16	57c N 32, 39
169	3c	944	15/09/16	57c N 26, 27
186	3c	924	15/09/16	57c S 12, T 7
186	3c	925	15/09/16	57c S 12, 6
191	9c	1762	15/09/16	57c T 20, 21, 26
191	9c	1764	15/09/16	57c T 3, 9
191	9c	1768	15/09/16	57c T 13, 19
191	9c	1769	15/09/16	57c T 8, 9, 10
191	9c	1772	15/09/16	57c T 7, 8, 14
191	9c	1773	15/09/16	57c T 1, 7, S 12
191	9c	1779	15/09/16	57c T 1, 2
191	9c	1781	15/09/16	57c T 2, 3, N 32
193	9c	1942	15/09/16	57c T 3, 4

Maps Used

GSGS 3062 1:10000 Combles Street 57c SW4 Edition 3A 30 August 1916
GSGS 3062 1:10000 Longueval Sheet 57c SW3 Edition 2F 9 September 1916
GSGS 2742 1:20000 France Sheet 57c SW Edition 3A 3 September 1916

VIMY RIDGE

9–10 APRIL 1917

The British attack in the Arras sector in April 1917 was intended to support a general attack ordered by Nivelle, by drawing away German forces from the Aisne. The Vimy Ridge battle was part of that often referred to as the Battle of Arras. The total frontage of the attack extended for about 15 miles, from Vimy Ridge to Croisselles, lying just to the south-east of Arras. The attacking forces comprised the Third Army under Allenby in the south and the First Army under General Horne in the north. The assault on Vimy Ridge itself was entrusted to General Julian Byng of the Canadian Corps, which was part of the Third Army. The battle is significant because the British preparation was thorough and included using tunnels and caves to bring troops to the front line unseen and in safety.

On Easter Monday, 9 April, the attack began at first light. The first assault wave of 20,000 men emerged from tunnels into driving sleet behind a rolling artillery barrage, and advanced on a front of almost 5 miles stretching from the right flank of the 1st Canadian Division to the Souchez River on the 4th Division's left. The Canadian Corps consisted of the 1st Division under Maj. Gen. Henry Burstall on their left with the 13th British Brigade. Next to them was the 3rd Division under Maj Gen Louis Lipsett, while the 4th Division under Maj. Gen. David Watson held the left of the line.

The plan for Vimy was in two stages. The 4th Division of the Canadian Corps with one brigade of the British 5th Division would attack on a 4-mile front, extending from Ecurie to Givenchy. The Vimy Ridge sector of the overall Arras battle plan was a protective flank for the Arras attack. Success at Vimy was therefore vital if the Arras attack was to have any chance of success. The northern end of the ridge, including the feature known as 'the Pimple', was one objective; the Bois en Hache, on the opposite side of the Souchez river from the Pimple, was to be attacked at the same time. The Canadian position meant that the troops at the southern end of the ridge would have to advance across some 4,000yds to reach their objective, while those at the northern end would have to cross only 700yds.

The German lines were heavily wired and strongly defended, with deep dugouts and concrete machine-gun emplacements. They offered a commanding view of the Canadian positions, and it seems very unlikely that the Germans were unaware of the Canadian preparations; unaccountably, however, they made no attempt to interrupt them.

The preliminary artillery bombardment was in two stages. Starting on 20 March, the bombardment opened at half strength, to delude the Germans as to the final intention. The main bombardment then started on 4 April to coincide with the Second Army's attack to the south. The amount of heavy artillery ammunition used in the preliminary bombardment was thirty times greater than that used by the French in their assault on the ridge in 1915, and in proportion to the extent of front involved, ammunition expenditure was more than double that used in the bombardment before the attack on the Somme on 1 July 1916.

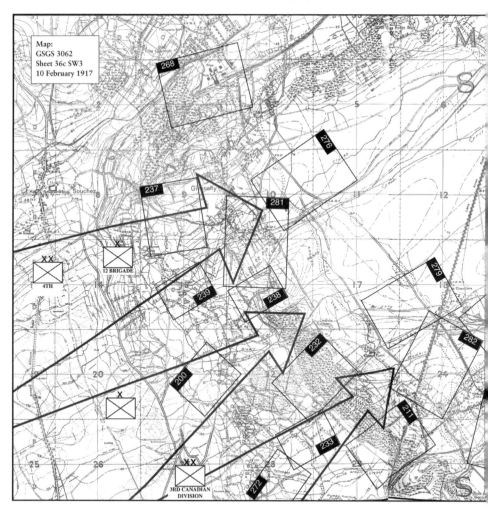

Map:
GSGS 3062
Sheet 36c SW3
10 February 1917

At 05.27 hours on 9 April, the gunners intensified the barrage into a 'hurricane' bombardment, which lasted three minutes. Then, at exactly 05.30 hours, the Canadians began their advance in driving sleet. The 1st and 2nd Divisions had the furthest distance to travel, and despite sustaining casualties from heavy machine-gun fire, they succeeded in capturing and crossing three successive lines of German trenches. By 07.00 hours the two divisions had achieved all their initial objectives and were now ready to push forward to the next: the village of Thelus and Hill 135.

At about 09.00 hours two fresh brigades, one British and one Canadian, spearheaded the assault on the two German divisions on Hill 135 and Thelus. Advancing behind a creeping barrage against sporadic resistance, the infantry captured the ruins of Thelus without much opposition and gained the ridge. At this point, the Canadian advance was checked as they had reached the limit of the

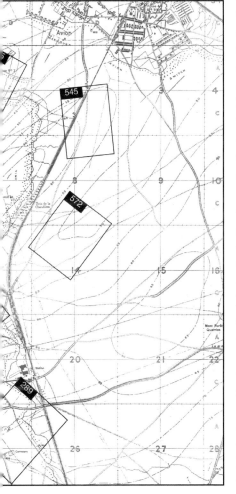

cover afforded by their heavy guns. Behind them the troops could see in great detail their own start positions among the churned-up morass of mud and shell-holes, while in front of them, beyond the German positions, they could see a countryside of villages and fields largely untouched by war. The divisions' victory was magnified by the number of German artillery batteries found abandoned in the woods on the slopes of the eastern edge of the ridge.

Meanwhile, the three divisions covering the centre of the ridge gained incredible success. The speed of their advance was such that they surprised and overran the Germans while they were still in their dugouts. The Canadians' initial objective was the Bois de la Folie, which ran along the western slope and crest of the ridge. This they reached but quickly met strong resistance inside the wood. Casualties soon began to mount and they were forced to start consolidating their gains in order to repel German counter-attacks.

Although the 4th Division had the shortest distance to advance, about 700yds, theirs was the most difficult task. Their objective was the highest point of the ridge, Hill 135, which was strongly defended. This strongpoint had not been bombarded by the artillery, because the infantry believed it would be useful once it had been captured. Surprise was an essential part of the plan to capture the position; the plan was successful on the right flank of the division's attack, but the centre met with strong opposition from the strongpoint where the wire had not been cut. Having sustained heavy casualties, the division was unable to make any further effective progress until the evening when it was reinforced by a support battalion.

On the left flank, the attack was held up only 200yds short of the summit, coming under heavy enfilade fire from the area of the Pimple. Thus by the end of the day the Canadians had achieved almost a total success, the only exception being at Hill 145, on the left flank, where they were forced to stop behind the summit.

During the night of 9 April, and into the early hours of the 10th, the 4th Division continued its assault on Hill 145. Gradually, the stubborn, courageous determination of the Canadian troops succeeded, and despite severe losses of about 13,000, including 3,000 killed, against the strong resistance of the German defenders, they captured the German position by the late afternoon. Thus the Canadian Corps succeeded in capturing and holding the strategically important feature of Vimy Ridge.

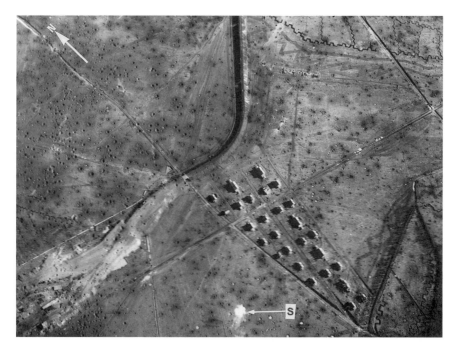

Print No. 173 5 April 1917 Height 3,700ft Scale 1:5500
Shell-burst (S) near the German second line on the outskirts of Vimy.

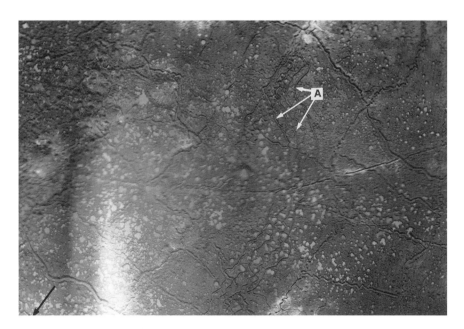

Print No. 200 6 April 1917 Height 3,000ft Scale 1:4500
This shows the wet conditions and water-filled shell-holes. The photograph includes the front line of the Canadian Corps and clearly shows the jumping-off trenches (A) prepared for the assault.

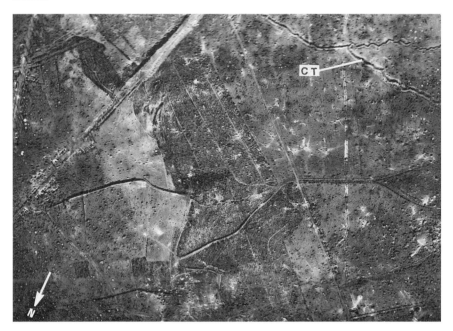

Print No. 211 6 April 1917 Height 4,000ft Scale 1:6200
This photograph shows the Prinz Arnolf Graben communication trench (CT), and the more open area in front of the Bois de la Folie.

Print No. 232 8 April 1917 Height 4,000ft Scale 1:6200
The Bois de la Folie through which the Canadians were to advance on the following day, with the German support trench (SP) annotated.

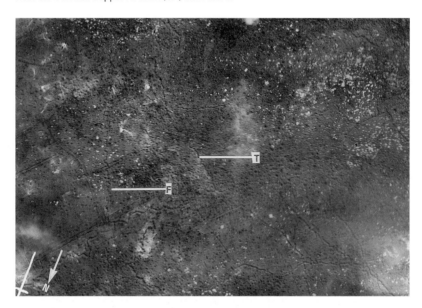

Print No. 233 8 April 1917 Height 4,000ft Scale 1:6000
This photograph shows the area over which the 3rd Canadian Brigade was to advance the following day. Although the print is of poor quality, the Zwischen Trench (T) can be identified. The conditions are wet and very muddy and the forward trenches are in a poor state so that Finckle Trench (F) has almost disappeared.

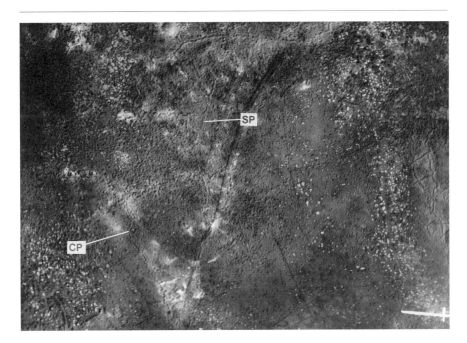

Print No. 237 8 April 1917 Height 3,700ft Scale 1:5600
This is the area just west of Givenchy. The outline of the road out of the village appears in an almost lunar landscape. The main trenches visible are the Clucas (SP) and Cluny (CP) German support trenches.

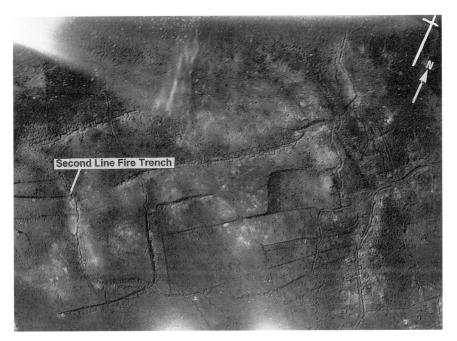

Print No. 238 8 April 1917 Height 2,600ft Scale 1:4000
This photograph shows part of the German second line on the 11th Brigade front.

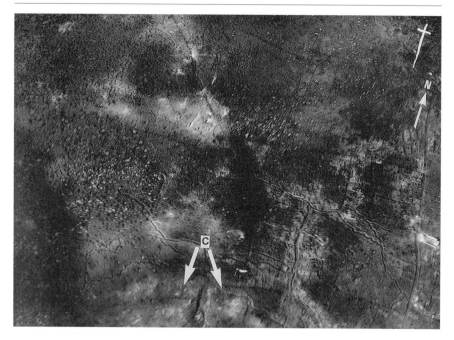

Print No. 239 8 April 1917 Height 2,600ft Scale 1:4000
This is part of the area of the 11th Brigade attack on the German first line. Although the print is of poor quality, the mine craters (C) show up clearly.

Print No. 268 8 April 1917 Height 4,600ft Scale 1:7000
Wrecked pit-head buildings at a mine north of Givenchy.

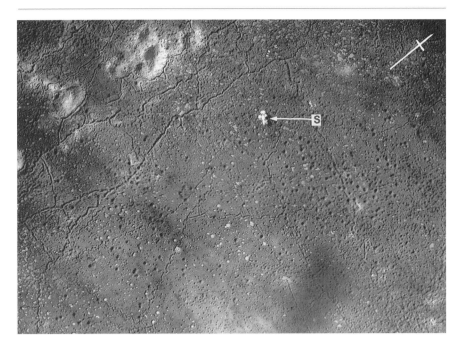

Print No. 272 8 April 1917 Height 3,000ft Scale 1:4400
There are mine craters in the top of the picture, together with a shell-burst (S).

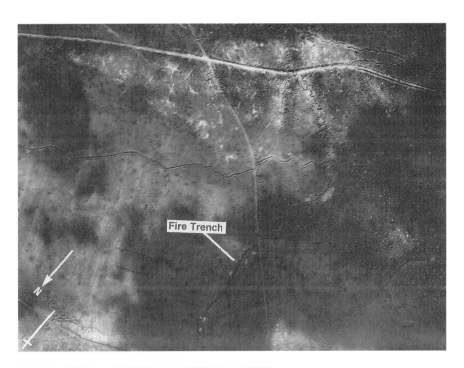

Print No. 276 13 April 1917 Height 4,600ft Scale 1:7000
The fire trench shown is part of the Vimy–Angres line, the German third line of defence.

Print No. 279 13 April 1917 Height 4,600ft Scale 1:7000
The ruins of the village of La Chaudière, on the Lens–Arras road. The communications trench
(C) running to the ruins suggests that they are probably defended.

Print No. 281 13 April 1917 Height 4,600ft Scale 1:7000
The print shows part of Givenchy. The main part of the village is in the centre of the print.
'Cyclists trench' (marked (C)) was part of the German second-line trenches.

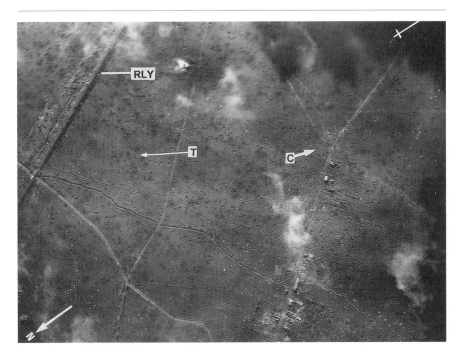

Print No. 289 13 April 1917 Height 4,600ft Scale 1:7000
This photograph shows the east side of the village of Vimy. The cemetery (C) has been obliterated. Shell-holes have been joined up to create a trench (T) in front of the railway embankment (RLY).

Print No. 282 13 April 1917 Height 4,600ft Scale 1:7000
On the right is the edge of the village of Petit Vimy, with a communication trench (CT) alongside the main Lens–Arras road.

Print No. 283 13 April 1917 Height 4,200ft Scale 1:6300
The remains of the devastated village of Vimy.

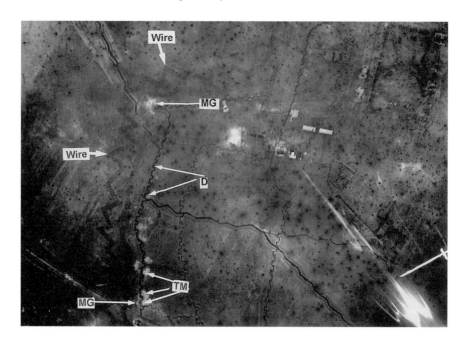

Print No. 495 24 April 1917 Height 3,600ft Scale 1:5600
This photograph shows a new German front-line fire trench in front of the village of Coulotte. Dark zigzags of wire can be seen. Fresh excavations indicate probable trench mortar (TM) and machine-gun positions (MG).

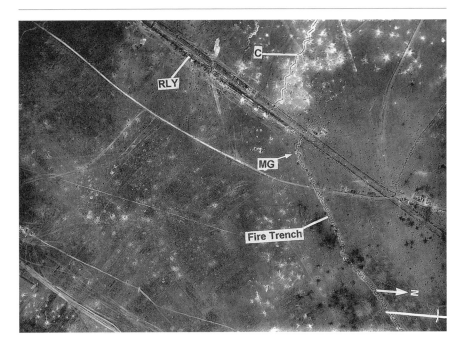

Print No. 545 24 April 1917 Height 4,000ft Scale 1:6000
This photograph shows part of the railway cutting south of Avion. There is a new fire trench with a probable machine-gun (MG) position and a communication trench (C) running from the railway cutting (RLY).

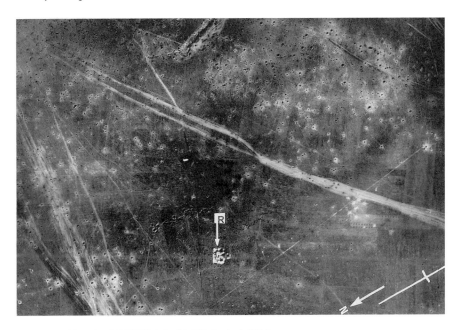

Print No. 572 24 April 1917 Height 4,000ft Scale 1:6000
This is a rear area, showing the ruins (R) of a large house. There are no signs of military activity near it although there are shell-holes and vehicle tracks on the road to either side.

DESCRIPTION FROM THE AIR PHOTOGRAPHY

The photography covers the period from 5 to 24 April 1917. While the attack took place on the 9th, no prints have been found for that date, so it is assumed that no reconnaissance was possible on the day itself when the weather was poor and probably unsuitable for air reconnaissance.

DETAILS OF PHOTOGRAPHS USED

Box	Series	Neg. No.	Date	Map Plot
408	16AB	71	05/04/17	36c S 1
409	16AB	200	06/04/17	36c S 21
409	16AB	211	06/04/17	36c S 29, 30
409	16AB	232	08/04/17	36c S 22, 23
409	16AB	233	08/04/17	36c S 28, 29
409	16AB	237	08/04/17	36c S 9
409	16AB	238	08/04/17	36c S 16
409	16AB	239	08/04/17	36c S 9, 15
409	16AB	268	08/04/17	36c S 3
409	16AB	272	08/04/17	36c S 28
409	16AB	276	13/04/17	36c S 10, 11
409	16AB	279	13/04/17	36c S 17, 18
409	16AB	281	13/04/17	36c S 10, 16
409	16AB	282	13/04/17	36c S 24
420	16AB	283	13/04/17	36c T 19, 25
420	16AB	289	13/04/17	36c T 25, 26
420	16AB	495	24/04/17	36c T 1
420	16AB	545	24/04/17	36c T 2, 8
420	16AB	572	24/04/17	36c T 14
881	16AB	173	05/04/17	36c T 13, 19

Maps Used
GSGS 3062 1:10000 VIMY Sheet 36c SW3 Edition 8A 10 February 1917

CAMBRAI

20–27 NOVEMBER 1917

The Battle of Cambrai was conceived originally as a raid in an area where the ground had not been damaged by artillery and where the going was suitable for tanks. In the autumn of 1917 the offensive north of Ypres petered out in the wet conditions, with high casualties. Cambrai seemed to offer the chance of a much-needed success to offset the costly failure of Passchendaele. The attack was to be made by III and IV Corps of the Third Army under General Byng, spearheaded by a mass tank attack of 474 Mk IV tanks. The tanks were to lead the battle, supported by six infantry divisions in the first phase. IV Corps would have seventy tanks with the 51st Highland Territorial Division and fifty-six tanks with the 62nd West Riding Territorial Division; their first objective was the village of Havrincourt, then they were to move on north-eastwards towards Flesquières.

On the left of the attack was IV Corps, with the 62nd Division and the 51st Division; on the right was III Corps, comprising the 20th Light Division, the 6th Division, the 12th Eastern Division and the 29th Division. In addition, IV Corps was to be assisted by the 36th Ulster Division and the 56th London Territorials. The divisions from V Corps, comprising the 40th, 59th and the Guards Division, were in reserve. The main attack was to come from III Corps with the 2nd and 3rd Tank Brigades. On the right, the 12th Division was to capture the Gonnelieu Ridge and the Lateau Wood while the 20th Division was to carry the attack from La Vacquerie to the Welsh Ridge and the Hindenburg support line. The village of Ribecourt and the eastern part of the Flesquières Ridge were to be taken by the 6th Division, while the 29th Division was to pass through both the 20th and the 6th Divisions to capture the high ground south of Ramilly and the Bois du Neuf (Nine Wood). Having seized this objective, three companies of tanks were to advance, seize and hold the bridges over the Canal de l'Escaut from Marcoing to Massières until the 29th Division arrived, so that the 2nd and 5th Cavalry Divisions could cross over.

The 1st Tank Brigade was allocated to IV Corps. The first objective of the 51st Division was the capture of the Flesquières Ridge and the village; then they were to capture the guns to the north, followed by the village of Cantaing. The 62nd Division on the left was to clear the Hindenburg support line up to the Bapaume–Cambrai road and capture the Canal du Nord bridge. It was then to capture Graincourt and Anneux, then assist the 1st Cavalry Division in taking Bourlon Wood, from where the cavalry was to advance north-west to Cambrai. Meanwhile the 36th and 56th Divisions were to hold the canal bridge on the Bapaume–Cambrai road and 'mop-up' west of Flesquières.

By 05.00 hours on the morning of the attack, the tanks were formed up some 500yds behind the British front line. Their first task was to cut paths through the

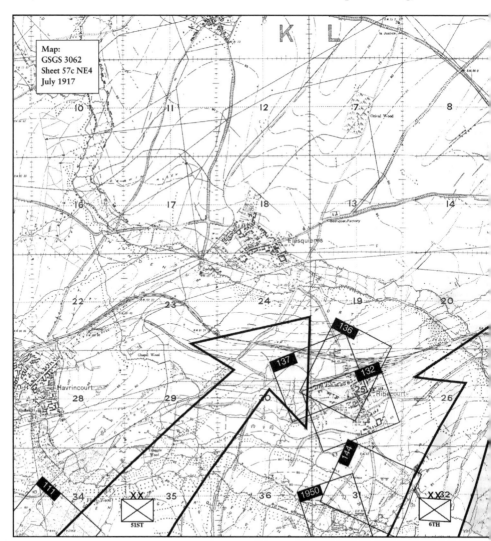

British wire ready for the assault. The country is perfect for tanks, being generally flat. On the British left the ground sloped down gently to Ribecourt and then gradually sloped upwards again to the Flesquières Ridge. Behind this the ground sloped upward to Bourlon village and Bourlon Wood. On the right the ground sloped down into a shallow valley which extends from the village of Villars-Plouich inside the British line, through the Hindenburg line to the villages of Marcoing and Masnières. Beyond this the ground sloped up to Cambrai. The German wire belts in front of the first Hindenburg line trench system were at varying distances across no-man's-land of up to 500yds.

On Tuesday 20 November, at 06.20 hours, the assault commenced with a 1,000-gun barrage as the tanks crossed into no-man's-land. At the same time,

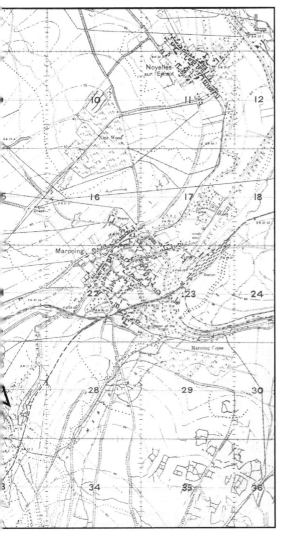

the 3rd Brigade Royal Flying Corps began ground attacks on German trenches to support the tanks and infantry. The tanks advanced on a broad front and by 08.00 hours the whole of the Hindenburg main line from Havrincourt to L'Escaut Canal was in British hands. Pockets of resistance remained. On the extreme right C and F Battalions, leading the 12th Division attack along the Bonvais ridge, were held up at Lateau Wood by a German battery including a 5.9 howitzer, but the battery was eventually overcome. On the left of the 12th Division, the 20th Division, led by tanks of I & A Battalions, advanced into the valley beyond the Gonnelieu spur and Welsh Ridge. In the centre, tanks of B & H Battalions spearheaded the attack of the 6th Division and took Ribecourt, but came under artillery fire from the direction of Flesquières. On the extreme left, the 62nd Division attacked the Havrincourt woods with the objective of Havrincourt village on the end of the Flesquières Ridge. The tanks were delayed by fallen trees and by artillery fire from a battery concealed behind the ridge, which put six tanks out of action before the village was taken.

By 11.30 hours the whole of the Hindenburg main and support lines on a 6-mile front had been captured. The only hold-up was at Flesquières in the centre of the front. Here four batteries of field guns deployed from concealed positions into the open to engage the tanks of G & E Battalions leading the 51st Highland Division as they crossed the ridge. Eleven of the fifty-six tanks were put out of action on the approach to the ridge and a further sixteen were destroyed as D & E Battalions crossed the ridge before the German battery was silenced. Although the 51st Highland Division outflanked and entered Flesquières village, the troops were forced to pull back after fierce fighting and the village was only taken after the Germans withdrew during the night.

The 62nd Division advanced with orders to take Graincourt and then Anneux, west of Bourlon Wood, and the bridges on the Bapaume–Cambrai road over the Canal du Nord. Graincourt was captured but after the cavalry had been help up at Anneux by machine guns, the division withdrew to Graincourt.

While IV Corps' advance faltered at Flesquières, the main attack of III Corps was more successful, advancing up to Masnières. By 15.00 hours the British line extended from Gonnelieu through Lateau Wood, Masnières (south of the canal), Marcoing, Nine Wood, Noyelles, Flesquières, to Graincourt, west of the Canal du Nord. The bridge at Masnières was destroyed, but others, as at Marcoing, were intact.

The 6th Division with fourteen tanks had reached Marcoing by 11.30 hours and began the house-to-house clearing of the village. A further fourteen tanks bypassed Marcoing, and reached Nine Wood a little before midday. At about the same time, the 87th Brigade reached Marcoing and crossed the canal by the railway bridge, with support from two tanks which arrived at Flot Farm, the 87th Brigade's final objective.

At this point, the 5th Cavalry Division was sent forward in support, its advance units reaching Marcoing at about 14.00 hours. As the cavalry began to cross the canal, they came under machine-gun fire and were forced to dismount. Additional infantry reinforcements were brought up to deal with continuing German resistance around Rumilly. This was successful, but the advance was delayed again outside Masnières by further German resistance. This proved difficult to overcome and with the onset of dusk, the attack ceased for the day.

During the afternoon, further units of the 1st Cavalry Division had reached Marcoing. Their task was to advance from the village and capture Noyelles, Cantaing and Fontaine, before reaching round to Bourlon. They reached Noyelles, which was then secured by the infantry by about 16.00 hours. Although some of the 1st Cavalry Division continued and actually reached Cantaing, they were held up by wire and machine-gun fire and had to retire.

In the IV Corps area, the attack was spearheaded by the 51st and 62nd Divisions, but the 51st Division's infantry were following too far behind the tanks in the attack on the Flesquières Ridge. By the late afternoon the German anti-tank batteries had been overcome and some tanks had entered Flesquières. However, these came under heavy fire from the German troops still in the village, and because the supporting infantry were too far behind to provide the necessary support, the tanks were forced to withdraw.

Meanwhile, both brigades of the 6th Division achieved their first objective by 09.30 hours and moved round Havrincourt, reaching their second objective against reduced resistance by 10.30 hours. The division's reserve brigade then passed through the two leading brigades to advance on to the Bapaume–Cambrai road, and then on towards Moeuvers. Supported by tanks and cavalry, the brigade crossed the Hindenburg support line and reached the edge of Graincourt. However, artillery fire knocked out all the six tanks in the advance, and another three tanks had to be brought up to knock out the guns before the infantry could capture the village. Although the leading brigade, the 186th, began to advance beyond Graincourt towards Anneux, the supporting cavalry were halted by machine-gun fire from Anneux, and the advance stopped.

During the evening of the 20th, the Third Army prepared to resume its attack on the following day. The III Corps sought to capture the Masnières–Beaurevoir line, in a joint action by the 20th and 29th Divisions, to secure the crossings of the St Quentin Canal for the cavalry. Early in the morning, while it was still dark, the 29th Division began to clear the houses in Masnières, and then continued towards the Masnières–Beaurevoir line; however, the troops met such strong resistance that they were delayed and missed the main assault, which was scheduled for 11.00 hours. At the same time the 20th Division began its attack at 06.30 hours, but heavy machine-gun fire stopped its advance on the canal bank, near Les Rues des Vignes. The infantry attempted to make further progress without tank support (the tanks had not yet arrived), but heavy enemy fire stopped them. A section of four tanks arrived after 15.00 hours, not having received any movement orders until after zero hour, but they did not cross the canal because of concerns about the strength of the bridge. East of Marcoing, on the bend of the canal, the 29th Division waited for the arrival of the eighteen tanks which crossed the canal on the railway bridge. The tanks then worked along the trenches, but were met by intense machine-gun and field-gun fire, which put three tanks out of action. The infantry could advance no further owing to the intense opposition and the advance had effectively ended for the day by 15.30 hours. While this was happening, the Germans were counter-attacking at Noyelles, but despite the determination of their attack, they were repulsed and then driven out of the village after fierce house-to-house fighting.

In the IV Corps area, Flesquières, which had been abandoned by the Germans overnight, was occupied by the 51st Division. The next objective was the village of Fontaine, about 3 miles from Cambrai. There was again a delay in sending for the tanks, so that the leading brigade, the 154th, went into action without their support and was subsequently halted by intense fire from the trenches at Cantaing. This also prevented the intended movement of the 1st Cavalry Division, which was to have skirted the village and then moved north. However, the arrival of thirteen tanks together with cavalry soon after midday enabled Cantaing to be occupied by 13.30 hours, and the infantry went on to capture Bourlon and Fontaine with the aid of four tanks. Both Bourlon and Anneux had been taken with the assistance of tanks, despite fierce resistance by the Germans. However, the sustained heavy fire from Bourlon Wood brought the advance effectively to a halt.

The main objective for the next day, 23 November, was the capture of the Bourlon Ridge. The attack was to be spearheaded by the 41st and 40th Divisions, the 40th having relieved the 62nd. The 40th Division was to take Bourlon Wood and Bourlon village itself from the south-west. At the same time, the village of Fontaine was to be recaptured by the 51st Division, which would then move on to Bourlon Wood, where the 1st Cavalry Division would threaten the village from the south-east. The attack was to be supported by ninety-two tanks, forty-eight with the 51st Division, thirty-two with the 40th and twelve with the 36th.

The attack began at 10.30 hours. The 51st Division advanced on Fontaine under artillery support. The tanks entered the edge of the village under intense machine-gun and anti-tank fire, but the supporting infantry were too far behind and no progress could be made. Additional tanks arrived in the afternoon, but the German defences had already been strengthened, and their defence held firm against the British attack. Meanwhile, the 40th Division reached the Bourlon–Fontaine road, and had reached Bourlon Wood with thirteen tanks by 13.00 hours, but were subjected to heavy artillery fire and forced to withdraw. However, a strong German counter-attack was repulsed.

On 24 November the 40th Division again attacked Bourlon village with twelve tanks and dismounted cavalry in support. There were two strong German counter-attacks during the morning and a third German attack pushed the British defenders of Bourlon Wood back, and the attack on the village was postponed to the next day, the 25th. However, the attempt to capture Bourlon village failed.

On 26 November, the British heavy artillery bombarded the areas of Fontaine, Quarry Wood and elsewhere, but not Bourlon because of its partial occupation by British troops. On the 27th the Guards Division, which had relieved the 51st Division, attacked Bourlon, but intense enfilade fire and a strong German counter-attack necessitated a fighting withdrawal to the division's start line. This failure to take Fontaine and Bourlon effectively ended the offensive.

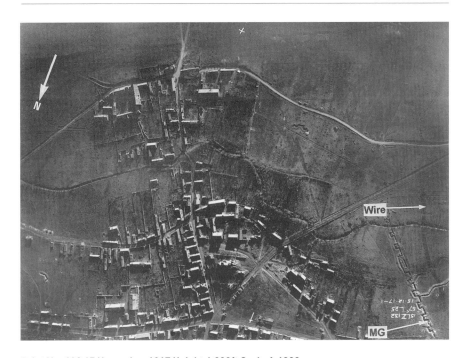

Print No. 132 15 November 1917 Height 4,200ft Scale 1:6300
The village of Ribecourt. The buildings appear largely undamaged. A probable machine-gun position (MG) and a covered dugout are marked.

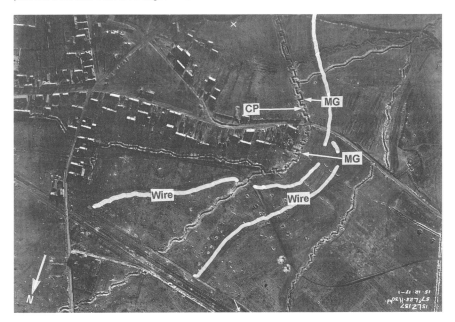

Print No. 137 15 November 1917 Height 4,000ft Scale 1:6000
The German defences around Ribecourt. Two probable machine-gun positions (MG) and a possible command post (CP) are shown.

Print No. 144 15 November 1917 Height 4,400ft Scale 1:6500
The German support trench (SL) with a machine-gun position (MG) in the area of the 6th Division front.

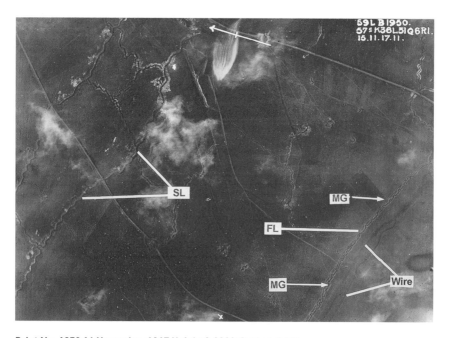

Print No. 1950 16 November 1917 Height 3,800ft Scale 1:5800
This photograph shows part of the area of the 6th Division front. It includes the German front-line fire trench (FL) and the support trench (SL). Wire is marked and possible machine-gun positions are also indicated.

Print No. 111 12 November 1917 Height 5,000ft Scale 1:6000
This print shows part of Havrincourt Wood, which was largely felled by the Germans. Felled trees (F) may be seen and a new trench (T).

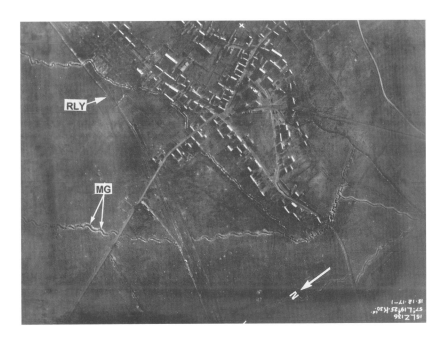

Print No. 136 15 November 1917 Height 4,000ft Scale 1:6000
The village of Ribecourt, just after the battle. Although of poor quality, close examination of this print reveals tracking, probably from tanks around the east side of the village (left on the print). Probable machine-gun positions are shown (MG).

DESCRIPTION FROM THE AIR PHOTOGRAPHY

There is very little photography in the archive from 16 November until well into December, and the photographs shown here illustrate what was available immediately prior to the battle.

DETAILS OF PHOTOGRAPHS USED

Box	Series	Neg. No.	Date	Map Plot
731	15LB	111	12/11/17	57c K 33, 34
737	59KB	1950	16/11/17	57c K 36
737	59KB	2087	19/11/17	57c K 8, 9
740	15KZ	132	15/11/17	57c L 25
740	15KZ	136	15/11/17	57c L 19
740	15KZ	137	15/11/17	57c L 25
740	15KZ	144	15/11/17	57c L 31
742	59LB	1951	15/11/17	57c L 22
742	59LB	1953	15/11/17	57c L 34
742	59LB	1968	15/11/17	57c L 26, 27

Maps Used
GSGS 3062 1:10000 Marcoing Sheet 57c NE4 Edition 4A July 1917

AMIENS

8 AUGUST 1918

At the end of July, the last major German attack in their salient to the east and west of Rheims failed. The Marne salient then ceased to be a threat to Paris but became a potential trap for the invading German forces. The French 10th Army struck the German flank with the assistance of the US 1st and 2nd Divisions and the 4th British Division. By the end of the first week of August, the Germans had suffered a major defeat, losing about 168,000 men. Meanwhile preparations were being made in the utmost secrecy for an allied attack on the Somme to push the Germans back from Amiens. The action was to be made by III Corps of the British Fourth Army on the north bank of the River Somme, securing the allied left flank, with the French 1st Army securing the right flank south of the Amiens–Roye road. Between III Corps and the French were the Australian and Canadian Corps.

Rawlinson's objectives, as given by Haig, included the line of villages that formed the old French front line known as the Amiens Defence Line at a maximum distance of 7 miles from the front line. The Australian and Canadian Corps were to make the main assault, with the left flank of the Australians resting on the Somme and the flank of the Canadians on the east–south-east railway from Villers Bretonneaux. Their objectives were 4 miles into the German defences.

The four Australian divisions under Monash were responsible for the segment between the River Somme and the Amiens–Nesle railways, while the Canadian divisions under Lt Gen Sir Arthur Currie held the area between the Australians and the French. Supporting the attack was a large tank force of 324 Mark V tanks with 184 supply tanks and two battalions of Whippet light tanks. Artillery support was provided by 700 heavy guns with about twice as many field guns.

On 6 August a surprise attack by the Germans disrupted the battle preparations. The British III Corps were pushed back and the troops had to fight hard to regain the ground, which they did on the following day. Despite the evidence indicating an imminent attack, not only in the ammunition dumps but also in the mixture of troops among the 200 or so men the Germans took prisoner, general security over the forthcoming battle ensured that the plans were not compromised. Thus the allied attack opened as scheduled at 04.20 hours on 8 August with a heavy but short artillery bombardment. The barrage lasted only three minutes on the targeted German batteries, before being lifted and moved forward by 100yds; at this point the infantry advance began.

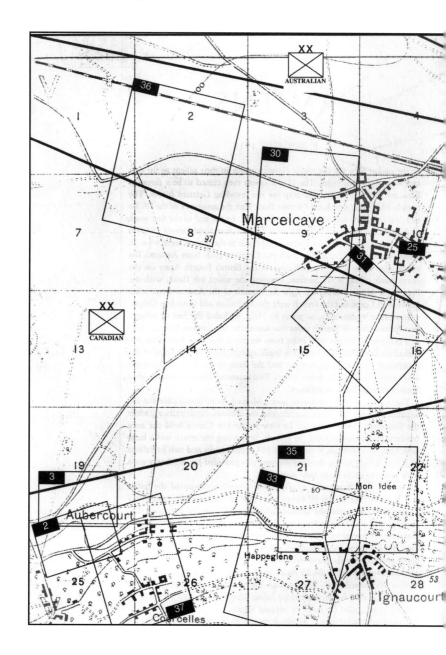

Despite the information gathered during their attack on the 6th, the Germans were apparently taken by surprise and the short hurricane bombardment of their positions gave them no time to prepare their defence. Moreover, the early morning mist helped obscure the advance and everything went according to the Allied plan. By 07.00 hours the Australian Corps had reached and taken its first objective, which was the ridge from Warfusée-Abancourt to Cérisy-Gailly

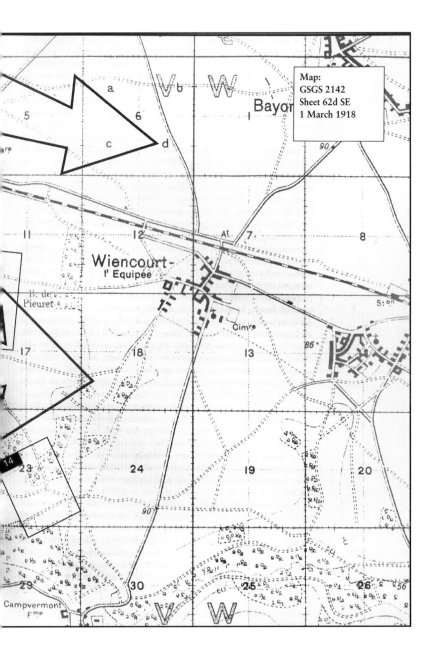

Map:
GSGS 2142
Sheet 62d SE
1 March 1918

near the river. The Corps then reached its second objective, which included the villages of Morcourt and Harbonnières by 10.30 hours. The Canadians also made a rapid advance from their starting positions slightly west of the Australian Corps, and were in position alongside the Australians by 11.00 hours.

Although the tanks performed well, there were considerable losses from enemy artillery fire, with many more lost to breakdowns or accidents. On the Canadian southern flank, at Le Quesnel, the tanks were reduced by artillery fire to a sole survivor. Meanwhile, the Australian advance on their northern flank was slowed owing to the British III Corps being unable to take their objective, the Chipilly spur, until the following day. However, by 13.30 hours the Allies had advanced further than planned, having covered between 6 and 8 miles. The cavalry and light tanks worked independently. Light tanks (Whippets) captured a four-gun field battery between Warfusée and Bayonvillers. Beaucourt and Santerre were taken by Canadian cavalry, and an 11ft railway gun and 600 prisoners were captured by the 5th Dragoons.

Ludendorff subsequently referred to 8 August as the 'Black Day of the German Army'. At the end of the day, the Canadians had captured some 5,000 prisoners and 161 guns, and the Australians 8,000 prisoners and 173 guns. British and Dominion losses totalled 6,500 killed and wounded. Total German losses numbered over 30,000 killed, wounded or captured.

In the Canadian Corps sector, south of the railway line, the countryside was generally open except for the occasional wood or village. Sir Arthur Currie, Commander of the Canadian Corps, put the 1st Division on the left and the 2nd on the right; each division was to advance on a frontage of one brigade, with the other two brigades ready to leapfrog through as each objective was captured. The Canadians had thirty-six tanks (new Mark Vs) with their 3rd Division, twenty-one with the 1st Division and seventeen with their 2nd Division. The tanks led the assault, which took place after a short and heavy bombardment, but they sustained considerable casualties. Of the twenty-eight tanks that initially crossed the river, eight were destroyed by anti-tank artillery and a further eight were ditched.

Tank losses were generally heavy. Out of 415 tanks that went into action on 8 August, over 100 were knocked out by German artillery and anti-tank rifles, and only 145 were ready for action on 9 August. In addition the cavalry lost about a thousand horses while the RAF lost forty-four aircraft with another fifty-two seriously damaged.

The success of the attack on the 8th was a complete surprise to the Germans; it also went far beyond what the Allies had expected, so that the subsequent plan to exploit the success was rather vague. At 04.30 hours the 4th Division began the assault of Le Quesnel, without artillery support but with the assistance of a few tanks, and forced the Germans out of the village, but they were not able to overcome the strong German resistance in the woods next to the village until the afternoon. The main attack was scheduled to start at 10.00 hours but poor communications delayed the assembly, causing the attack to be postponed by an hour. These various delays meant that the start of the advance was piecemeal, with only one brigade out of the five involved actually crossing the start line on time. This brigade, the 6th, belonging to the 2nd Division, went into action without tank support, while the brigade next to them started to move company by company rather than en masse. On the right, the 1st Division was also late starting because the artillery was late into its positions, and the division did not commence its advance proper until 13.00 hours. This generally slow start meant that the forward elements of the 4th Division did not reach Le Quesnel until 14.00 hours.

Meanwhile, the Germans had reorganised their defences and the numbers of the defenders now equalled the numbers of attackers. Although their positions were poorly fortified, many of them had natural strength. In the Canadian area, the country was fairly open, but there were five villages across the Canadian Corps' path, with others beyond and with numerous groups of farm buildings about a mile apart. This open ground gave little cover for the attacking force, but offered wide sweeping fields of fire for the German machine guns. The Canadian divisions had only limited artillery support, but they did have some effective help from a few Mark V and Whippet tanks. Although the cavalry were present, there was little opportunity for them. By advancing in short rushes, and making use of all the available cover, the Canadians were able to push forward and enter the villages. The village of Rosières was captured by part of the 2nd Division by 16.30 hours after some difficult street fighting, and the loss of four of the five supporting tanks. The rest of the 2nd Division advanced up a flanking valley beyond Rosières to capture Méharicourt. At the same time the 1st Division made a 3-mile advance to Rouvroy, capturing three other villages on the way. On the right wing the 3rd Division, which had made a late start, advanced along the main road and reached Bouchoir. As the Canadians advanced, the Australian Corps kept pace with them and reached the Lihons Ridge, in line with the Canadian position.

The Canadian advance had inflicted heavy losses on the Germans, effectively routing two of the divisions brought up from their reserves.

General Rawlinson's plan for 10 August was similar to that of the previous day; in other words, the men were to press on, on a wide front, with the Canadian Corps as the spearhead. In a dawn attack the 3rd Division launched the Canadian Corps' general attack and took Le Quesnoy beyond Bouchoir. To help the momentum of the attack, GHQ released the 32nd Division from the reserve; these fresh troops passed through the 3rd Canadian Division and, supported by tanks, captured two woods, although they were pushed out of the second by a strong German counter-attack. At this point, German resistance was stiffening, and the going was becoming more difficult as the battle was now entering the area fought over in 1916. The ground here was a mass of old shell-holes of all sizes; old trenches and wire, all now overgrown with grass and brambles, making obstacles difficult to see, especially from a distance.

Supported by sixteen tanks, the 4th Canadian Division started after the 32nd Division and made good progress, enabling squadrons of the 2nd and 3rd Cavalry Divisions to move up and capture the village of Andréchy, together with the supply depot which was located there. However, with enemy opposition hardening, the Canadians managed only with difficulty to gain the villages of Fouquescourt, Chilly and Hallm, and then struggled to hold them against strong German counter-attacks. The Australians at the same time faced similar difficulties, with their 1st Division progressing only half a mile to take and hold a small wood against determined counter-attack.

On 11 August General Rawlinson issued orders – against his better judgement – in compliance with the directive of Marshal Foch, to advance to the Somme canal, a distance of 8 miles. At dawn the 1st and 3rd Australian Divisions resumed their assault and gained the whole of the Lihon feature, together with the village, and repulsed the counter-attack of a fresh German division. However, the Canadians were not so successful. The 32nd Division had little artillery support and sustained heavy losses, including nine tanks, for an advance of only half a mile towards the village of Roye. At this point General Rawlinson, convinced that Marshal Foch's directive was misguided, issued orders to stop further attacks by both the 32nd and 4th Divisions. He believed that before they could contemplate any further advance the men had to be rested, and plans made to prepare and coordinate a fresh assault which, he suggested, could take place on 15 August. Field Marshal Haig supported his decision, and the Battle of Amiens ended with great gains in ground and captured men and materials.

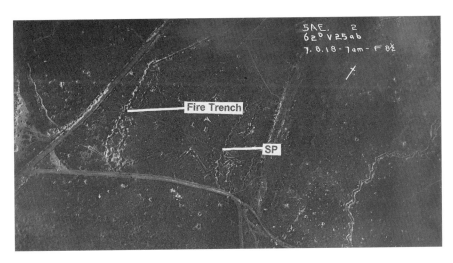

Print No. 2 7 August 1918 Height 3,400ft Scale 1:4800
This photograph shows the defences near the western edge of Aubercourt. There are newly dug trenches by the main road, with communication trenches. The fire trench is annotated, as is the support trench (SP). The trenches are not continuous, indicating that the war had become more mobile, and trenches are being used for specific defensive positions rather than for general defence.

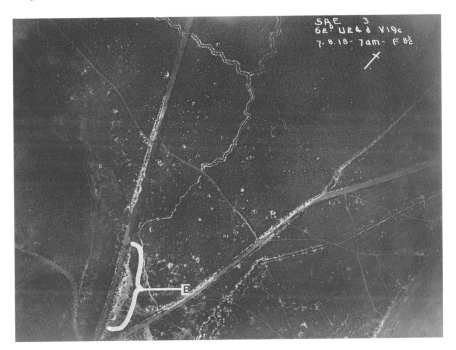

Print No. 3 7 August 1918 Height 3,400ft Scale 1:4800
Further trenches to the north-west of Aubercourt. Possible road blocks (B) have been created by felling trees along the road. (Shelling has apparently not defoliated the trees, as it is unlikely that tree trunks would throw such clear shadows.)

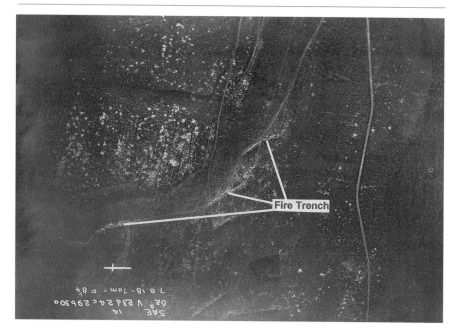

Print No. 14 7 August 1918 Height 3,600ft Scale 1:5200
Only short stretches of fire trench are to be seen in this heavily shelled area east of Ignaucourt.

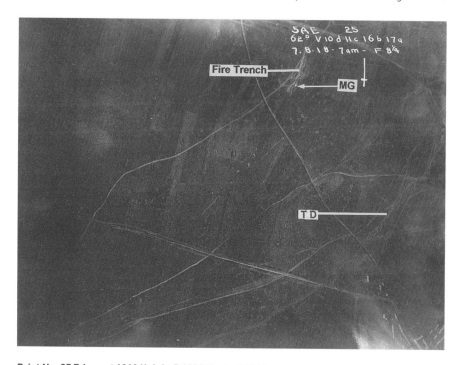

Print No. 25 7 August 1918 Height 5,100ft Scale 1:7200
German defences east of Marcelcave, including an abandoned trench (TD). An active fire trench is shown, with a probable machine-gun position (MG).

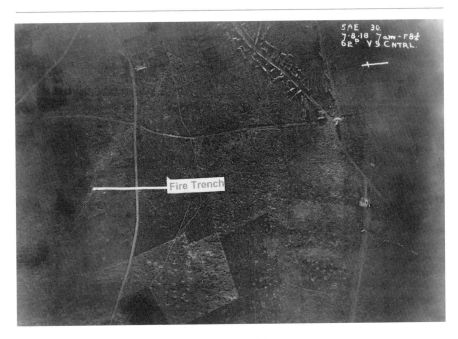

Print No. 30 7 August 1918 Height 5,100ft Scale 1:7200
Fire trench to the north-west of Marcelcave.

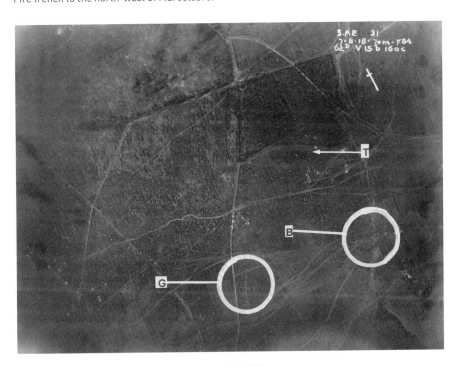

Print No. 31 7 August 1918 Height 5,100ft Scale 1:7200
The area to the south of Marcelcave. A possible shallow fire trench is shown at (T). Probable artillery positions are at (G), with a second probably abandoned position at (B).

Print No. 33 7 August 1918 Height 6,200ft Scale 1:8800
This photograph shows the west edge of Ignaucourt. No defences can be seen.

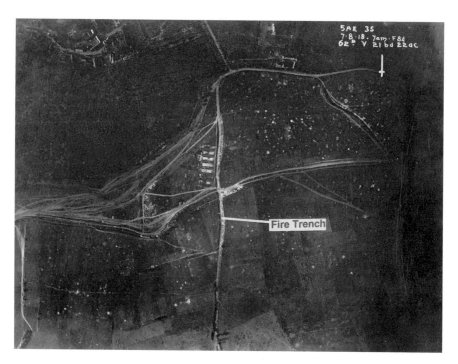

Print no. 35 7 August 1918 Height 6,200ft Scale 1:8800
This photograph shows fresh excavations, probably for a new fire trench.

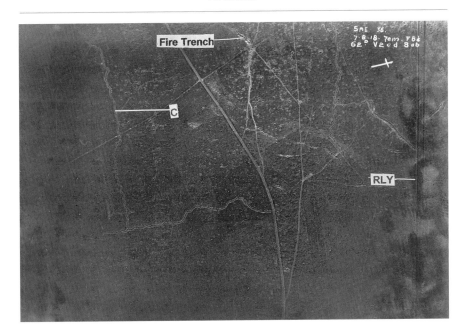

Print No. 36 7 August 1918 Height 6,200ft Scale 1:8800
This print shows the railway (RLY), which was the Corps boundary between the Canadian and Australian Corps. All the trenches have been recently dug, and a fire trench and a communication trench (C) are marked.

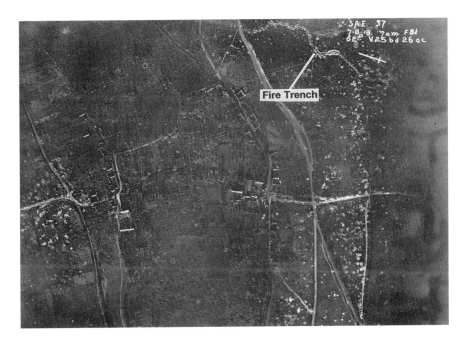

Print No. 37 7 August 1918 Height 6,200ft Scale 1:8800
Abercourt and Courcelles. New fire trenches have been dug on the western edge of Abercourt. No defences can be seen at Courcelles.

DESCRIPTION FROM THE AIR PHOTOGRAPHY

Following the German attack in March 1918, the central area of the British lines were forced back over the Somme battlefields, so that all the ground that had been so painfully won over the previous three years was lost. But as the German advance lost momentum the Allies counter-attacked, successfully forcing the Germans back. The nature of the war now changed from the static positions of entrenched warfare to one of comparative mobility. This is clearly shown on the air photography in preparation for the Battle of Amiens. The deep and extensive trench systems are no longer seen, and defensive activities take on a more modern look. Trenches are comparatively short, without the details of permanence, such as concrete emplacements and deep dugouts. Wire is no longer seen in thick belts, while machine guns tend to be in open emplacements for easy movement.

The objectives of photographic Intelligence Officers in the second half of 1918 would increasingly be to find where the retreating enemy was mounting a defence, and particularly where his artillery positions were so that they could be engaged by the Allied artillery.

DETAILS OF PHOTOGRAPHS USED

Box	Services	Neg. No.	Date	Map Plot
1130	5AE	2	07/08/18	62D V 25
1130	5AE	3	07/08/18	62D V 19
1130	5AE	14	07/08/18	62D V 23, 24
1130	5AE	25	07/08/18	62D V 10, 11, 16
1130	5AE	30	07/08/18	62D V 9
1130	5AE	31	07/08/18	62D V 15, 16
1130	5AE	33	07/08/18	62D V 27
1130	5AE	35	07/08/18	62D V 21, 22
1130	5AE	36	07/08/18	62D V 2, 8
1130	5AE	37	07/08/18	62D V 25, 26

Maps Used
GSGS 2142 1:20000 FRANCE Sheet 62d SE Edition 1 March 1918

THE HUNDRED DAYS

The Hundred Days campaign has been included for comparison purposes. Following the success at Amiens, there was a period of consistent advance which pushed the German army back and forced the Armistice in November. This period of hard fighting broke out of the trench fighting of the previous three years and brought a return to open, mobile warfare. The two prints shown illustrate the change in warfare. The countryside is open, and trenches are not held in depth. The annotations are those applied in 1918, and no modern annotations have been added.

Print No. 57M D551 5 October 1918 Height not known Scale not given
This photograph shows the increasingly open countryside with few trenches as the German army was steadily pushed back. The area shown is east of Lesdain, which is near Rumilly on Map 57 Bnw3.

Print No. 57M D984 1 November 1918 Height not known Scale not given
This photograph shows the woods and open fields with no military activity visible. The position is Jenlain, which is west of Mordain and appears on Map 51A on the 40,000 series, as no 10,000 series map was apparently available.

BIBLIOGRAPHY

Battlefields of the First World War (T. & V. Holt, 1995)

Bloxland, Gregory, *Amiens 1918* (Frederick Muller, 1968)

Brown, Malcolm, *IWM Book of the Somme* (Sidgwick & Jackson, 1996)

Brown, Malcolm, *IWM Book of the Western Front* (Sidgwick & Jackson, 1993)

Chasseaud, Peter, *Trench Maps – A Collector's Guide* (Mapbooks, 1986)

Clark, Alan, *The Donkeys* (Hutchinson, 1961)

Cooper, B., *Ironclads of Cambrai* (Souvenir Press, 1967)

Eaton, H.B., *APIS – Soldiers with Stereo* (Private Publication, Intelligence Corps Museum, 1976)

Farrar-Hockley, A., *The Somme* (Batsford, 1954)

Finnegan, Terrance J., *Shooting the Front* (The History Press, 2011)

Fletcher, David, *Tanks and Trenches* (Sutton Publishing, 1994)

Gilbert, Martin, *First World War Atlas* (Routledge, 1994)

Holmes, Richard, *War Walks* (BBC Books, 1995)

Johnson, J.H., *Stalemate: Great Trench Warfare Battles 1915–1917* (Arms & Armour, 1995)

Levine, Joshua, *On a Wing and a Prayer* (Collins, 2008)

Lewis, Cecil, *Sagittarius Rising* (Warner, 1994)

Macarthy, Chris, *The Somme: the day by day account* (Greenwich Editions, 1993)

Notes on the Interpretation of Aeroplane Photographs (HMSO, 1916)

Official History of the War: Military Operations, France and Belgium 1915: Vol. 11 (Macmillan, 1928); *1916: Vol. 1* (Macmillan, 1932); *1917 Vol. 11* (HMSO, 1948)

Stedman, Michael, *La Boisselle* (Pen & Sword, 1997)

Warner, P., *The Battle of Loos* (William Kimber, 1976)

INDEX